Cambridge Elements ≡

Elements in Ancient and Pre-modern Economies
edited by
Kenneth G. Hirth
The Pennsylvania State University
Timothy Earle
Northwestern University
Emily J. Kate
The University of Vienna

A HISTORICAL ETHNOGRAPHY OF THE ENGA ECONOMY OF PAPUA NEW GUINEA

Polly Wiessner
University of Utah

Akii Tumu
*Director Enga Taake Anda, Tradition
and Tradition Centre*

Nitze Pupu
*Enga Taake Anda, Research Director, Tradition
and Transition Centre*

CAMBRIDGE
UNIVERSITY PRESS

CAMBRIDGE
UNIVERSITY PRESS

Shaftesbury Road, Cambridge CB2 8EA, United Kingdom

One Liberty Plaza, 20th Floor, New York, NY 10006, USA

477 Williamstown Road, Port Melbourne, VIC 3207, Australia

314–321, 3rd Floor, Plot 3, Splendor Forum, Jasola District Centre,
New Delhi – 110025, India

103 Penang Road, #05–06/07, Visioncrest Commercial, Singapore 238467

Cambridge University Press is part of Cambridge University Press & Assessment,
a department of the University of Cambridge.

We share the University's mission to contribute to society through the pursuit of
education, learning and research at the highest international levels of excellence.

www.cambridge.org
Information on this title: www.cambridge.org/9781009485951

DOI: 10.1017/9781009368773

When citing this work, please include a reference to the DOI 10.1017/9781009368773

First published 2024

A catalogue record for this publication is available from the British Library.

ISBN 978-1-009-48595-1 Hardback
ISBN 978-1-009-36876-6 Paperback
ISSN 2754-2955 (online)
ISSN 2754-2947 (print)

A Historical Ethnography of the Enga Economy of Papua New Guinea

Elements in Ancient and Pre-modern Economies

DOI: 10.1017/9781009368773
First published online: May 2024

Polly Wiessner
University of Utah

Akii Tumu
Director Enga Taake Anda, Tradition and Tradition Centre

Nitze Pupu
Enga Taake Anda, Research Director, Tradition and Transition Centre

Author for correspondence: Polly Wiessner, pollywiessner@gmail.com

Abstract: The question addressed in this Element is: What happens to a society when, in the absence of influence from foreign populations, constraints are released by a new crop, making possible significant surplus production? We will draw on the historical traditions of 110 tribes of the Enga of Papua New Guinea recorded over a decade to document the changes that occurred in response to the potential for surplus production after the arrival of the sweet potato some 350 years prior to contact with Europeans. Economic change alone does not restructure a society nor build the social and political scaffolding for new institutions. In response to rapid change, the Enga drew on rituals that altered norms and values and resolved cultural contradictions that inhibited cooperation to bring about complexity rather than chaos. The end result was the development of one of the largest known ceremonial exchange systems prior to state formation.

Keywords: pre-state exchange systems, evolution of complex institutions, rituals and economic coordination, oral traditions as history, Enga of Papua New Guinea

ISBNs: 9781009485951 (HB), 9781009368766 (PB), 9781009368773 (OC)
ISSNs: 2754-2955 (online), 2754-2947 (print)

Contents

Introduction

In 1985, Akii Tumu and I set out to record the oral historical traditions of some 110 tribes of Enga. I was a researcher at the Max Planck Institute for Human Ethology in Germany and Akii was the director of the Enga Cultural Center in Wabag, Papua New Guinea (PNG). Akii knew it was the eleventh hour to record the rich body of historical traditions that were no longer passed down in men's houses. We thought we would complete the work in two or three years; nearly forty years later, we are still learning. If we had known just how much work would be involved, we probably would not have had the heart to start, but the engaging puzzle of Enga precolonial history kept us going over the many steep and slippery ridges of the Enga landscape to reach knowledgeable elders from all tribes. When we returned many times to try to further our understanding, some asked, "Haven't you two been at this for a long time (and still not figured it out)?" Some arduous trips yielded little; others opened new horizons. We were joined by Nitze Pupu, the first blind lawyer in PNG; Pesone Jarwe Munini, who covered religion in the past; and Alome Kyakas, who researched women's lives.

It is hard to know where to begin with the distribution of thanks. First of all, we would like to thank the hundreds of elders who generously gave us their time and expertise, realizing the importance of passing on knowledge of Enga culture. The contributions of some are cited in this Element and many more in the acknowledgments in *Historical Vines* (Wiessner and Tumu 1998). Nitze Pupu and Akii Tumu carried out the majority of translations, though others assisted. Many thanks go to researchers and missionaries who gave us photos of Enga life shortly after contact, which bring much of the text to life, and to Dawn Farkas for producing the maps. The better part of this work was funded by the Max Planck Institute for Human Ethology with the understanding of the late Professor Eibl-Elbesfeldt concerning how long such research takes. The Enga Provincial Government has worked with us and assisted with essential advice, infrastructure and staffing over the past nearly forty years. We are extremely grateful to the hundreds of elders, colleagues and institutions who helped us. Many of the testimonies in this Element are abreviated from those in *Historical Vines*.

1 The Enga: Their Economy and Historical Traditions

> The great Pendaine was dressed to perfection from head to toe with his skin glistening under the mid-day sun . . . Because of his tall stature, his plumes seemed to reach the sky. It was a dazzling, spectacular sight . . . All eyes were fixed upon him, and as the expression goes, even the frogs down by the Lai river stopped croaking . . . Pendaine's line of stakes was the longest of all.
>
> (Kopio Toea Lambu, Timali Clan, Lenge, 1987, on the life of Pendaine, the renowned Tee Cycle organizer)

Every person has something of value and must be treated with respect. Even a person who brings fleas into the house may be of value one day because the flea bites might wake you when your life is in danger. (Kekeo Yapao, Sikini Wapai Clan, Lakopena 1988, quoting his mother Takime, one of the few prominent female Tee Cycle organizers)

1.1 The Questions

What happens when people in a small-scale society with strong principles of equality are first able to produce a storable surplus has engaged archaeologists, anthropologists and economists for decades. For the majority of human history, people lived as hunter-gatherers, developing the wide array of cognitive capacities and motivations we possess today. However, climate, environmental conditions and corresponding social dependencies to cover risks exerted limits on production and the expression of many human motivations. The stabilization of climate during the Holocene over the past 10,000 years (Richerson et al. 2001) allowed for surplus agricultural production that in turn released many economic constraints.

Archaeologists have carried out extensive and insightful research providing evidence that storable surpluses transformed economic production, retention and distribution; increased population growth; fueled the expansion of larger political units; and accentuated social inequalities and economic specialization (Boone 1992; Clark and Blake 1994; Earle 1997; Flannery and Marcus 2012; Graeber 2011; Hayden 2001; Johnson and Earle 2000; Price 2021). Paths to building social, political and economic advantage have been shown to be highly variable with actors deploying different combinations of strategies involving wealth in people, wealth in knowledge and wealth in things (Guyer 1995; Guyer and Belinga 1995). However, there is only so much that can be deduced from material remains alone. Missing is an understanding of the institutions necessary for social transformation (Brumfiel 1992; Furholt et al. 2020). These include how collective action was organized for larger sociopolitical enterprises (Wiessner 2019), and how internal conflicts were resolved, emotions coordinated, new motivations evoked, goods valued, emerging social inequalities masked and differential governance orchestrated from both the bottom up and top down.

Enga oral history provides an unusual opportunity to understand the dynamics of the economic, social and political changes that arose with the potential for surplus production (Map 1). Some 400 years ago, before European contact, the sweet potato was arguably brought from South America to Indonesia by European explorers (Ballard et al. 2005). It spread through the local trade to arrive among the Enga of highland PNG during a period of famine (Wiessner 2005). Sweet potatoes released constraints on production, allowing Enga to

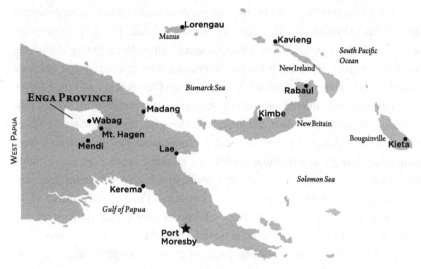

Map 1 Location of Enga province in Papua New Guinea

gradually settle more permanently, practice more intensive agriculture, expand into higher-altitude areas and produce a substantial surplus "on the hoof" in the form of pigs (Watson 1965, 1977). Far-reaching networks of social, economic and ritual interaction developed. So great was the flow of wealth and information within and among these networks that they were restructured with each generation (Wiessner and Tumu 1998). One outcome of economic growth was the Tee Ceremonial Exchange Cycle, which incorporated some 40,000 people in 355 clans and tens of thousands of pigs by the time of first contact with Europeans (Meggitt 1974).

Fortunately, elders still remembered a factual body of oral traditions recording the history of each Enga tribe and its constituent clans, ordered by genealogies and extending back at least nine to twelve generations. These oral histories were systematically transmitted in men's houses, covering almost all aspects of life, including individual experiences (Lacey 1975; Wiessner and Tumu 1998). The course of events Enga historical traditions describe presents an unusual state of affairs: the sweet potato was introduced within the span of historical traditions some 350 to 450 years ago, but the arrival of the first Europeans occurred only within living memory, briefly in the 1930s, but largely after World War II. The Enga oral record thus allows us to work with questions that usually lie beyond the reach of ethnohistorians and evade archaeological analysis of material remains. What happens to a society when, in the absence of influence from foreign populations, production possibilities are released by a new crop and significant surplus production becomes possible?

Our intent in this Element is to use two perspectives to address these processes of surplus production and increasing economic and political complexity: a historical ethnography and an anthropological history. We begin by identifying some of the historical forces behind economic and demographic change that were originally set off by the arrival of the sweet potato (Brookfield and White 1968): population growth, altered subsistence strategies, new potential for wealth production and resulting warfare and migration. However, understanding the forces that generated change is not sufficient to understand how these forces were structured through new cultural institutions to bring about complexity rather than chaos. The perspective from anthropological history addresses how new integrative institutions emerged from former ones as Enga drew on rituals of the spirit world, feasting and ceremonial exchange to reset values, preferences and motivations and to resolve internal social contradictions. These innovations provided the infrastructures for new forms of cooperation, promoting economic growth and developing economic inequalities.

The starting point is a subsistence-based economy with a big-man or transegalitarian political system in which position is attained and maintained by attracting supporters (Hayden 1995; Sahlins 1963). Big men have the influence to bring about changes but neither power over others nor the ability to transmit position. Motivations and initiatives coming from those on top are evaluated and approved or rejected in clan meetings to create a current of change from above and effective governance from below (Ostrom 1990). The central thesis is that the forces of social selection (Hrdy 2016; Nesse 2010) in a big-man society required leaders to develop new institutions that would provide benefits and engage large segments of the population, setting off rapid growth in the surplus economy and increasing social complexity. The resulting economic competition and growth eventually caused the vast institutions governing warfare, ritual and exchange to be constantly modified so as not to collapse under their own weight. The discussion starts around the time of the arrival of the sweet potato, circa 350–400 years before the present, when the Enga relied on basic horticulture and hunting and gathering. Our end point is the establishment of Australian colonial administration and missions throughout Enga in the 1950s and 1960s, launching a fascinating but entirely different trajectory of change.

1.2 Background

When we began our research in 1985, the roads and paths of Enga led us on a journey through diverse terrains, each challenging the foot or wheel in a different way. Traveling from the east to the west, the road led down the steep, narrow valley following the Minamb river into the lush rolling valley of the Lai (ca. 1,700 m altitude). There the landscape was a patchwork of houses, small trade stores, flourishing gardens, casuarina forests, grasslands and ceremonial grounds with their ancient trees (Figure 1). After passing Wabag (1,850 m) in central Enga, the valley narrowed and the road climbed into the high, open and starkly beautiful grassland of Sirunki (2,600 m) that separated the valleys of the Lai and Lagaip. It descended rapidly to Laiagam (2,200 m), where the headwaters of the Lagaip converged to form a basin that seemed to contain a whole world within its mountain walls. The characteristic Enga gardens, houses and ceremonial grounds were similar in many respects throughout Enga, but there was not the same feeling of abundance in these high, steep valley settlements of the Lagaip. The road continued down the Lagaip valley for some forty kilometers to ascend Mt. Maip and then descended steeply into the Porgera valley (2,200 m). Porgera was a melting pot of Enga, Ipili and Huli communities now transformed by one of the world's largest gold mines. The north–south road from Laiagam to Kandep (2,200+ m) climbed out of the valley, over a mountain pass and down into the Kandep area with its vast, high-altitude grasslands and swamps. Signs of prosperity were evident only in the longhouses constructed for pig exchanges and the monstrously large pigs that emerged from the swamp grasses. It was hard to imagine that such a diversity of landscapes could be the home of some 500,000 people who share a single language and cultural institutions.

The Enga who inhabit this country are a highland agricultural population settled between approximately 1,200 and 2,600 meters. Fleeting contact with gold prospectors in the major valleys occurred around 1934 and was followed by

Figure 1 Enga house surrounded by gardens. Mounds for sweet potato cultivation in the background (courtesy of Don Jeffers, mid-Lai valley, 1966)

the arrival of the Taylor and Black patrol from the Australian administration, which set up a patrol post and airstrip at Wabag in 1939. From 1942 until the end of World War II, the Wabag post served to keep lines of communication open, although the war had little impact on Enga other than delaying colonization (Lacey 1982). When the war ended, patrol posts and missions were established throughout Enga. The colonial administration appointed local leaders, established a police force and the Australian legal system, and tried to end warfare, while missionaries simultaneously established churches, schools, agricultural projects and clinics. In 1975, after PNG became independent, Enga was declared a separate province. Most of the economic history discussed in this Element occurred prior to European influence, except that discussed in Sections 9 and 10.

Virtually all aspects of more traditional Enga life have been described in the anthropological literature. The publications of Meggitt cover most geographical areas, including social organization and economy (1956, 1958, 1965a), *tee* ceremonial exchange (1972, 1974), gender (1964b, 1990), religion (1965b), leadership (1967) and warfare (1977). The studies of Waddell (1972) and Wohlt (1978) provide a sound understanding of Enga agricultural systems. Other important works cover Enga religion (Brennan 1977; Feacham 1973a; Gibbs 1977, 1978); Tee Cycle (Bus 1951; Elkin 1953; Feil 1982, 1984, 1987); women's lives (Kyakas and Wiessner 1992); environment and health (Feacham 1973b); oral traditions (Lacey 1975, 1979, 1982; Wiessner and Tumu 1998) and warfare (Young 2004). The characteristics of Enga society discussed next, described in the past tense, are those that prevailed shortly after contact with Europeans. Although some practices have changed, many persist.

The Enga population was divided into nine mutually intelligible dialect groups that shared many aspects of economic, social, political and ritual life (Map 2). Regular exchange of trade goods, ideas, practices and rituals with all surrounding linguistic groups occurred throughout the period covered, particularly with the Mandi, Huli, Kakoli and Kyaka. Boundaries with surrounding groups were open and no interlinguistic group hostilities enter into historical traditions. The Enga were horticulturalists who relied on the cultivation of the sweet potato in an intensive system of mulch mounding to feed large human and pig populations. Other traditionally cultivated crops included yams, taro, bananas and sugarcane. Nutritionally rich pandanus and other forest foods supplemented the diet; marsupials and cassowary were frequently hunted.

Political units were defined by a segmentary lineage system that divided groups into tribes, clans, subclans and lineages, each with its own big men. At the time of Meggitt's studies in the 1950s and 1960s, tribes of central Enga were composed of between 920 and 5,400 people divided into an average of 7.8 clans with a range of 100–1,000 members each (Meggitt 1965a). Tribes and clans shared a common

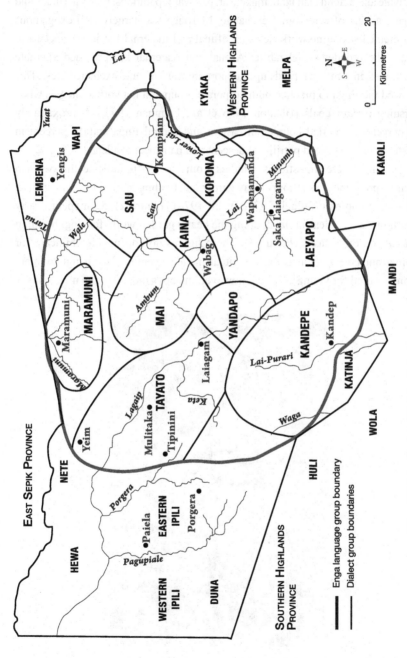

Map 2 Mutually intelligible dialect groups in Enga province (Brennan 1982)

origin myth and genealogy that linked male members to the legendary tribal founder. The central corporate group was the clan whose members cooperated to cultivate and defend clan land, make war, pay war reparations, perform rituals and stage festivals of ceremonial exchange. Marriage was largely clan exogamous and created strong network ties with affinal and maternal kin in other clans to weave the broader social fabric. Affinal and maternal kin provided alternate residences in times of hardship, support in warfare and exchange ties. This allowed the Enga to practice both corporate group and network strategies when pursuing certain goals (Blanton 1996 et al.; Feinman 1995). Approximately 90 percent of married couples in eastern and central Enga and 70 percent in western areas practiced patrilineal descent and patrilocal residence.

The Enga were industrious. Studies from the 1970s indicate that women spent approximately six hours a day gardening, tending to pigs and carrying out household chores (Waddell 1972; Wohlt 1978) (Figure 2). Men spent nearly four hours a day clearing land, doing the heavy garden work, fencing, building houses and other tasks (Figure 3). These figures do not include childcare for women and engagement in warfare, ritual and *tee* ceremonial exchange for men. Women cared for young children; however, the boys moved to the men's house

Figure 2 Woman in garden with small child and pig (courtesy of Rev. Otto Hintze, Yatamanda, early 1950s)

Figure 3 Men building a traditional house (courtesy of Paul and Ruth Wohlt, Yumbisa, northern Kandep, 1973)

at the age of six to eight years. Women raised the pigs that were the foundation of the household wealth; a large pig was the product of five or more years of feeding and care.

Male–female relations were characterized by a separation of the sexes that was more pronounced in western Enga than in eastern Enga owing to beliefs about the dangers of menstrual contamination for men. This created major contradictions within Enga society: male–female separation was essential for male secrecy and unity in times of warfare, while ties with affinal and maternal kin were key to most forms of external cooperation and exchange. Gender divisions were strengthened by separate men's and women's houses. Though Enga adults of the same sex were initially considered equals, men competed to become leaders or big-men by displaying skill in mediation, oration and wealth management to provide benefits for their fellow clan members. Women did not engage in overt competition, though their accomplishments in the private realm as producers and the active links between clans were acknowledged (Kyakas and Wiessner 1992). Men's status in relation to other men was achieved with backing from their wives and female kin, though the separation of men and women was set by ideology.

Politics occupied much of men's time and effort. Whereas frequent and destructive warfare created sharp divisions between clans and claimed the lives of 15–25 percent of the male population (Meggitt 1977; Wiessner 2010b), women departed with the pigs and children at the onset of war and were rarely targets of violence (Kyakas and Wiessner 1992; Meggitt 1977). Compensation exchanges of pork, live pigs, shells, salt, oil and foodstuffs were used to reestablish peace. Ceremonial *tee* distributions of wealth demanded the continual supervision of men as well as the attention and diplomacy of the women who formed bridges between groups (Feil 1978; Kyakas and Wiessner 1992). Cosmology and religious beliefs were dominated by two sets of spirit beings: the sky people and their descendants the ancestors.

1.3 Oral Traditions As History

History underlaid all matters of public concern and surfaced continually in public forums. It gave people a sense of identity and security as part of a larger group and thereby made them willing to make sacrifices for the group. Land disputes could not be resolved outside of their historical context; the settlement of wars hinged to a large degree on the history of relations between opposing groups. Historical knowledge was and is an important source of power and influence for Enga people. It was imparted to male clan members informally in the men's houses; those who sought more active public roles continually built upon this corpus of knowledge whenever opportunities arose. With the absence of men's houses today, it is no longer systematically transmitted. Historical information was contained in a variety of Enga oral traditions, so it was intriguing to work out what we could learn from different sources drawing on the insightful work of Roderic Lacey (1975; 1979).

1.3.1 Origin Traditions and Genealogies

The Enga distinguished between myths (*tindi pii*) and historical narratives (*atome pii*), although the two are entwined in origin traditions. Most tribal histories began with origin myths that provided markers for shared identity: the names of tribal founders and their spouses, places of origin and past economy. All tribal origin traditions included genealogies linking the narrator to the tribal founder, covering ten to fourteen generations. Genealogies established social and political divisions, tied groups to certain tracts of land and specified relations to one or more other tribes. Genealogies could be divided into two periods: the first covered the earliest two or three generations recording fictive ancestors who were representative of tribes and clans. We called this period "the founding generations." The second period began with the generation of subclan founders, from approximately the seventh generation

Table 1 Timeline showing major developments in Enga history

Generation 12-10	Introduction of sweet potato.
	Time of darkness, *yuu kuia* (mid-1600s).
	Hunting and gathering 2000m+.
	Taro/shifting horticulture1500–2000m.
	Thriving trade.
Generation 8	Populations shifts in response to sweet potato.
	Beginning of early Tee Cycle.
Generation 7-6	Large wars: population redistribution.
(ca. 1795–1855)	Kepele rituals spreads in western Enga.
	Sangai rituals arise in central Enga and spread.
	Ambum wars.
	Beginning of Great Ceremonial Wars.
Generation 5	Peace-making: war reparations paid to enemy.
(ca. 1855–1985)	Tee Cycle and Great Wars expand.
	Kepele (Aeatee) brought to central Enga.
Generation 4	Tee Cycle and Great Wars joined.
(ca. 1885–1915)	Aeatee used to merge Tee Cycle and Great Wars.
	Sangai spreads eastward, called Sandalu.
Generation 3	Tee Cycle takes over Great War routes.
(ca. 1915–1945)	1934 first contact with Europeans.
	1939 Taylor establishes base camp at Wabag.
	ca. 1940 Last Great War fought.
	1943–5 Ain's cult.
Generation 2	Colonial era: government posts & missions established:
(ca. 1945–1960)	1938–9 Wabag; Wapenamanda 1949-50; Laiagam 1952;
	Kandep 1960 (Lacey1982).
	Expansion of Tee Cycle.
Generation 1	Last Tee Cycle. Independence 1975.
(ca. 1975–2005)	

before the present until the generation of the narrator. Here the names of real people are documented (Wiessner and Tumu 1998). We defined generation one to be 1975–2005, the adult lifetime of most informants (Table 1). We were able to use genealogy to establish a chronological framework to order past events, because events could usually be placed within the lifetime of a person in the genealogy. Genealogies can also be used to trace the growth and dispersal of tribes to estimate population size (Lacey 1975; Wiessner and Tumu 1998: ch. 1).

1.3.2 Historical Narratives

Historical narratives had neither mythical qualities nor formal structure. They made up the greater part of oral traditions departing from myth and legend around the seventh generation before the present. They contain information on subsistence, the economy, warfare, migrations, major cults and the formation of ceremonial exchange networks. In the past, they were passed on in men's houses and were called on actively during clan meetings and other circumstances. The Enga sought to reproduce historical traditions as accurately as possible, though details from the earlier generations have been forgotten. If the narrator got something wrong or bent the tradition to suit his interest, others corrected him. This meant that versions of a given historical event collected in different clans of a tribe or across tribes rarely contradicted one another on major points.

Historical narratives did not seem to be revised to legitimate current interests. Rather, the whole body of traditions was retained so that elders could open the section of their history that best fit their current designs, leaving other traditions to be called upon when conditions change. We covered the history of 110 tribes of Enga in our research between 1985 and 1995 in order to look for consistencies between clan and tribal histories and to put together coherent histories on different topics. A number of other oral traditions contained valuable information: songs associated with certain events, magic formulae, praise poems from bachelors' cults, other rituals and adages. Enga historical traditions provided views from those at the top, middle and bottom of society, giving an unusual opportunity to understand the complex dynamics between people in different positions in the economic, social and political hierarchies. It is with these oral historical traditions, together with the research of others, that we will trace the post–sweet potato developments among the Enga.

2 Baseline: Environment, Population and Economy in the Early Generations

> Potealini met the wandering Mandi Sakalini who had made his way up from the southern Kandep area and asked him, "Brother, from where did you come?"
>
> Mandi answered, "I have been wandering around up there in the high country."
>
> "It's good that you have come. We'll make gardens and stay here together. Why don't you go out and hunt possums, birds and cassowaries and I will stay here and make gardens."
>
> Upon hearing this Mandi took his walking stick and planted it in the fence around the Potealini men's house at Kubalisa. That is how they spent their time.
>
> (Lanyia Kingi, Lyipini clan, Rakamanda, 1986)

Oral traditions from the founding generations of tribes depict a sparsely populated landscape with vast tracks of uncleared land. Immigrant groups were readily welcomed, distances between settlements were greater than they are today, and spouses were difficult to find. Nonetheless, by approximately 250 to 300 years ago, all central valleys of Enga, some adjacent high country and the southern region around Kandep were inhabited by small groups who intermarried, traded and participated in joint feasts and rituals. This had probably been the situation for thousands of years as was the case throughout much of the PNG highlands (Swadling et al. 2008). In this section we present information compiled from the early historical narratives on population, subsistence bases and agricultural production systems for various regions of Enga (Wiessner and Tumu 1998) to provide a baseline from which to look at subsequent changes.

2.1 Population, Production and Subsistence

In the founding generations (Table 1), Enga tribes were said to have been small with constituent clans composed of a few men's houses and their associated women's houses, locations of which are sometimes recalled. From genealogical information, we estimate Enga population size in the seventh generation to be approximately 10,000–20,000 in contrast with the 150,000 counted in the 1980 census, a growth rate of 1 per cent per annum in contrast to more than 2.3 per cent in recent decades (Wiessner and Tumu 1998: 56, note 7:431).

Table 2 summarizes the subsistence activities by area described in early historical traditions. The fertile lower valleys of eastern Layapo Enga were the most hospitable in the province before the arrival of the sweet potato. They were high enough, between 1,500 and 1,900 meters, to be above the malaria belt but low enough to permit reliable cultivation of such crops as yams, winged beans, bananas and sugarcane. Mid-valley slopes were kept for pig forage and the high forest for hunting and gathering. Pigs enter into a few traditions but they are in the background. Trade in salt, axes, shell ornaments and cosmetic tree oil adds intrigue to historical narratives of this era. Early historical narratives of eight groups from surrounding higher-altitude areas paint quite a different picture having hunting as their focus. This conforms to the pattern found throughout Enga – pre–sweet potato groups in higher altitudes focused on hunting and those from lower altitudes concentrated on gardening (Wiessner and Tumu 1998). Crops cultivated include taro, sugarcane, yams, bananas and greens. Crops mentioned include taro, sugarcane, yams, bananas and greens.

Central Enga, home of the Mai, Kaina and Yandapo Enga, offered both stretches of fertile garden land in the fertile Ambum valley below 2,100 meters and an abundance of wild cassowaries, possums, other marsupials and highly nutritious pandanus in the adjacent high country of Sirunki and the Yandapo. Here attention shifts to hunting; narratives indicate that a man of worth could provide his family with an ample supply of meat. Specific foods are mentioned in five origin traditions – taro, sugarcane, greens and wild pandanus. Pigs receive little notice.

For western Enga, historical traditions tell a different story. In the high country of western Enga at 2,100 to 2,600 meters lived mobile groups largely dependent on hunting and gathering; historical narratives do not mention any horticulture for these groups. Hunters were said to have great physical strength and ritual powers. Shifting horticulturalists, who raised a few pigs and engaged in some hunting and trapping, inhabited the narrow valleys below. Historical traditions and myths from western Enga depict culturally recognized distinctions between hunters and horticulturalists with hunters having a somewhat higher status. These groups intermarried and exchanged, but stories of their relationships are filled with tension and misunderstanding. Shifting horticulturalists of the Lagaip valley traded with groups far to the north for sago and with hunter-gatherers at higher altitudes for meat and forest products. In the Porgera valley the division between hunters and gardeners was similar to that of the Lagaip. Seasonal pandanus harvests provided an opportunity for people from neighboring linguistic groups – Enga, Huli and Ipili – to meet.

Moving south to the Kandep region of Enga, most of the land is above 2,300 meters and susceptible to occasional frost. Hunting, harvesting pandanus and foraging for wild foods are central to subsistence. When gardening is mentioned, it is in the histories of tribes of southern Kandep who had access to land in lower valleys. Pigs, which could be raised on forage in the swamps, receive considerable attention (Table 2). Food exchanges and feasts between people living at different altitudes were important throughout Enga history as a leveler of variation in food supply. Pandanus, taro and yams feasts gathered people for ritual purposes or merely to share a bumper harvest. Cult performances drew people from near and far with participants contributing the specialty foods from their areas for feasting. When frost affected higher-altitude areas, people there sought refuge in the lower valleys, where they were welcomed by their hosts. Frost refugees reciprocated when the forest provided an abundance of pandanus nuts or by contributing labor to their hosts' projects (Wohlt 1978).

Table 2 Subsistence practices mentioned in early historical traditions

	Eastern Enga	Central Enga	Lagaip	Kandep
Hunting/trapping	4	11	10	8
Gardening	16	8	5	6
Pigs	6	5	3	12
Wild pandanus	2	5	8	6

2.2 The Spirit World

Prior to the seventh generation, beliefs and practices for the spirit world exhibited the greatest cultural differences that existed between eastern/central and western Enga. Two beings stood at the center of all Enga cosmology: the immortal sky people (*yalyakali*) and the ancestors (*yumbange*). The sky people, who were attributed with control of natural events, were not linked to any specific social groups but were believed to assist in divination (Meggitt 1965b: 108) and helping youths reach maturity. Feasts were held to communicate with them, even though humans were believed to have little influence over their somewhat capricious ways.

Unlike the sky people, the ancestors were directly associated with maintenance of clan and tribal land, influencing soil and human fertility and assisting in defense. In the east and center, the ancestors were thought to reside in sacred *yainanda* stones, the fossilized bones of the ancestors (Swadling et al. 2008). When crops, pigs and children fared poorly or wars took a turn for the worse, a clan-based ceremony was held to communicate with the ancestors, provisioned by contributions of pork, marsupials and vegetable foods from all families in the clan. Food was distributed freely in order to underwrite equality and unity, and not used for economic ends. There is no mention of rituals for sacred stones in early historical narratives from western areas of Enga. The most widely performed ritual in western Enga was the *yaka kaima*, a fearsome ceremony held to ward of sickness – particularly leprosy – greet the *yalyakali*, appease angry ancestors and bring better fortune to the clan. The *yaka kaima* fit the needs of smaller mobile groups, for ancestral pools were said to appear near to their new settlements.

2.3 Trade

It is uncertain how ancient trade is in the PNG highlands, but archaeological evidence suggests it has a long history (Swadling et al. 2008). For at least

10,000 years, shells have been traded from the coast into the highlands (Hughes 1977). From the early generations of historical traditions, the Enga appear to have been an open society with widespread traveling, trade, experimenting and exchange of ideas. Emphasis was on give and take, not wealth accumulation. The "gold" of Enga was salt concentrated in the salt springs of central Enga (Meggitt 1958).

> The pack of traditional salt opened up areas such as the Layapo, the Sau, Kandep and regions to the west. The salt brought us the stone ax and its binding materials, cosmetic oil, *itatu* fruits (*Pangium edule*), along with fibers for making women's net bags and men's aprons. I was told by my father that if you do not have anything to do with the salt trade, then you will not meet new people bringing the goods that you yourself cannot produce here. (Ambone Mati, Nemani clan, Kopen, 1991)

Salt was made by soaking billets of soft, dried wood in saltwater pools for two to four months and burning the billets to ash that comprised the salt. Portions of saltwater pools were owned by individual families (Figures 4 and 5). Nonetheless traders from all over Enga and surrounding linguistic groups could easily obtain salt and sell it elsewhere at a profit (Wiessner and Tumu 1998). The area surrounding the salt springs was a peace zone – it was forbidden for residents or visitors to assault men who came to trade.

Figure 4 Salt springs fenced into squares owned by individual families (courtesy of Rev. Otto Hintze, Minamba Valley, 1950s)

Figure 5 Man with a packet of salt (courtesy of Rev. Otto Hintze, Yatamanda, 1950s)

Enga salt was traded for stone axes, marine shells, tree oil, net bags, tobacco, black palm, plumes and pigs. Most high-quality axes used to clear forests for gardens were obtained in the trade from quarries in the Waghi and Jimi valleys (Burton 1989). Wealthy families were the only ones able to acquire stone axes from the Waghi valley, which they occasionally lent to fellow clan members in exchange for small gifts. Inferior axes were made from local river stones. Tree oil that made the skin glisten in dances (*sing-sings*) was obtained from the Lake Kutubu region, where it was tapped from large lowland forest trees and transported north by Huli or Mandi traders. Other trade goods included black palm for aprons and net bags made by women from tree fibers, drums, shell ornaments, pigments and plumes. The value of items traded was established on the basis of: (1) production time, effort and skill; (2) utility and beauty; (3) difficulty to obtain and (4) culturally defined value. Several items of lower value could be combined to purchase those of greater value and vice versa (Meggitt 1974: 170).

Trade was carried out by middlemen or on trading expeditions. However, a central trade alliance of big-men (*kamongo*) from Tambul on the border of easternmost Enga to Tetemanda in central Enga controlled the flow of salt and axes. These networks carved out paths for high-volume exchange systems to emerge.

> Trade was done with members of Yanaitini, the Itokone, Yambatane and Yanuni tribes, all of whom had easy access to each other's resources. People from surrounding areas would bring trade goods to their relatives in these

tribes, giving what they had to offer in exchange for what they wanted to obtain. Arrangements were usually made through kinship connections. (Tipitape Kaeyapae, Itokone tribe, Pompabus, 1987)

2.4 Leadership

From the earliest Enga historical traditions, Enga appears to have been a transegalitarian or big-man society with contradictory ideologies: all individuals within genders were considered equal, yet men were expected to strive to become leaders of their clans or subclans (Boehm 2009; Godelier and Strathern 1991; Hayden 2001; Sahlins 1963; Wiessner 2002). Considerable variation exists in transegalitarian institutions in different societies (Crumley 1995; Fenton 1998; Harrison 2006; Hayden 2011; Leach 1954; Leacock 1978; Tuzin 2013; Uchendu 1965). They can grow to be complex and far reaching, though often their history can be reconstructed only through oral or archaeological records (Arnold 2005, 2010; Johnson and Earle 2000; Vansina 1990).

Numerous men of status and influence are mentioned in early Enga historical traditions: great cassowary hunters, ritual experts, warriors, big-men or *kamongo* who led local groups. Great hunters of cassowary – large, dangerous flightless birds – were prominent in groups inhabiting the high country for their ability to provide quantities of meat that could be shared widely. Ritual experts held specialized knowledge passed from father to son, though they were considered too odd and fearsome to translate their wealth and knowledge into other arenas of influence. War leaders were highly respected during times of conflict but not highly influential at other times. It was the big-men who exerted the most power to shape events by delivering eloquent speeches, organizing events, mediating conflicts, assisting group members economically and building exchange networks. Nonetheless, early big-men are portrayed as having a more muted style of leadership lacking the flamboyant displays of later generations. Most big-men engaged in polygynous marriages to expand their spheres of influence supported by ambitious, hard-working wives (Kyakas and Wiessner 1992).

2.5 Property Rights: Land

Land was owned both individually and corporately by the clan. It was passed from father to son, or in some cases, to daughters' descendants. Land could not be given outside the clan; infringement from neighboring clans on the land of a clan member was taken as an act of aggression against the entire clan. However, because labor, not land, was short, families often welcomed migrants who joined the clan in the early generations or gave land won in war to allies. Influential leaders could not acquire more land than the average clan member; rather they gave out some pigs on agistment.

2.6 Warfare

War has been part of Enga life since the beginning of historical traditions some 400 years ago and most likely long before that. Histories do not glorify war but describe it as an unfortunate last resort when problems could not be resolved; war heroes are not remembered or celebrated. This is in part because Enga wars were largely between neighboring clans who were also the ones who provided wives and assistance in times of peace; their support was costly to lose. Of thirty-one descriptions of pre–sweet potato wars, twelve triggering incidents were over hunting or sharing meat, fourteen were over possessions or sharing work, one was over pigs, one was over pandanus, one was over homicide/political provocation, two were over women and none were over land (Wiessner and Tumu 1998: 144). This contrasts with triggers for wars from the seventh to fourth generations when homicide/political provocation and land disputes most frequently set off wars. Of course, the incidents that set off wars do not convey underlying goals and tensions. Intra-tribal wars were sparked when communities grew too large to cooperate, but relationships of cooperation were usually reestablished some years after dispersal. Intertribal wars had more serious outcomes, continuing until one party was ousted to a remote portion of tribal land or to reside with relatives living elsewhere.

2.7 Summary

The pre–sweet potato population of Enga encompassed groups living very different lifestyles, from agriculture in the lower fertile valleys to hunting and gathering in the high country of western Enga. Nonetheless, the Enga form the largest of more than 800 linguistic groups in PNG despite occupying a complex geography and a range of economies. Why? Nothing in historical traditions suggests that the Enga migrated from another area or originated in a central area of Enga and subsequently spread out over the landscape. The answer may lie in a number of factors. Marriage rules were strictly exogamous and complex enough to ensure that unions forged advantageous external ties (Meggitt 1964a). Dependencies between groups stemming from the variation in subsistence base encouraged exchanges of foodstuffs between areas and alternate residences in times of frost, drought or war. The salt–stone axe trade formed an east–west axis that integrated different groups, while the trade for cosmetic oil and other products from lower altitudes created the same along the north–south axis. With the exchange of material goods came the exchange of ideas during rituals, feasts, compensation payments to allies in warfare and funeral gatherings.

3 The Arrival of the Sweet Potato in Enga: Repercussions

Mapu Takame
Cannot live without sweet potato

The arrival of the sweet potato in Enga is recorded in a historical narrative told by Pastor Alo Pitu, who traveled widely and collected narratives to satisfy his own interest (Wiessner and Tumu 1998). The story began with two sisters and a brother living near the coast in east Sepik who were mistreated by the community when their parents died. They packed up their possessions, including sweet potato vines, and struck out in the direction of Enga. They settled in the mountains of Hewa country, planting ample sweet potato and other crops and supplying people up the valley with sweet potato vines. An Enga hunter came down from the Lagaip valley near Walia in northwest Enga (Map 3), marveled at the lush sweet potato gardens and tried sweet potato for the first time. Later he brought the sisters and their sweet potato vines to his home in the Lagaip valley. The sisters planted sweet potato at Walia, where it grew well. Once sweet potato was abundant, the sisters held a distribution of sweet potato vines to surrounding groups, a practice mirroring traditional harvest feasts.

The credibility of parts of the legend is supported by the fact that it was commemorated in a ritual feast called Aina Pungi Toko – the bridge of the sweet potato vines – held from the early generations until the 1950s at sites extending from Walya in western Enga, down the Lagaip valley and on to the Tetemanda in the Lai valley (Map 3). The ritual was held when food shortages and flash floods occurred, indicating that the mythical women were signaling their desire to cross the creek to bring sweet potato and other foods to the male ancestors. People then constructed a bridge bedecked with sweet potato vines and feasted (Wiessner and Tumu 1998).

Although debate exists concerning how the sweet potato reached the New Guinea highlands, there is little doubt that it made a significant impact, releasing constraints on production and permitting demographic and economic growth (Ballard et al. 2005; Golson 1982; Watson 1965, 1977; Yen 1974). Most likely it was brought from South America to Indonesia by Portuguese explorers and passed via the local trade to New Guinea to arrive some 250–400 years ago (Ballard et al. 2005; Swadling et al. 2008). How the sweet potato was received in Enga depended heavily on existing subsistence regimes. Throughout western Enga, most early narratives mentioned that it rescued people from famine sparked by frost and drought. The tradition of the wandering women bringing the sweet potato, recalled in the Aina Pungi Toko rituals, extends into central Enga, where there are descriptions of experimentation with the new crop. By contrast to western and central Enga, no evidence indicates that the sweet potato was quickly accepted as a staple crop in the garden regime of the eastern Enga.

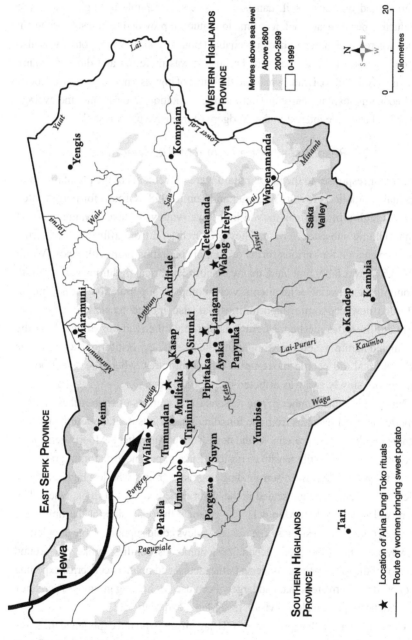

Map 3 Arrival of the sweet potato and Aina Puingi Ritual sites

Acceptance of the new crop was slower because taro and yams already provided a reliable subsistence base.

The new crop had a strong impact on the Enga economy because it grew at higher altitudes and on poorer soil than taro, was less susceptible to blight, was more productive per acre and took less time to mature. It provided secure subsistence in areas where gardening had been unreliable (Bourke 2005). Sweet potato was also a superior food for pigs than taro because it was preferred and did not require cooking (Hide 2003). Leaders realized the value of pigs as a new currency for social and economic exploits early on, but historical traditions indicate that the average household had little interest in the drudgery of intensive pig husbandry.

3.1 Responses to the Arrival of the Sweet Potato

The major responses to the sweet potato were movements of the population and gradual population growth (Wiessner and Tumu 1998). Groups formerly settled in most high-altitude areas moved into lower valleys to take advantage of the high-yielding subsistence base. They procured land from affinal and maternal kin in exchange for various forms of support including help with labor (Wohlt 1978), as it was labor, not land, that was short. Historical traditions indicate both economic and social adjustments were complex – population redistribution afforded new economic opportunities but also incited tension as people of different lifestyles meshed. Migrations disrupted the relations of people to the social and natural resources stimulating the rise of new institutions. Only as the valleys filled did people move up to higher altitudes, where the sweet potato grew more slowly and was affected by periodic frost.

Table 3 gives the number of and reasons for migrations of entire tribes or clans reported in tribal histories from the founding generations until the fourth and fifth generations before the present. We did not ask about wars after the fourth generation because some were still sensitive. Eastern Enga experienced the immigration of some forty-nine clans from surrounding linguistic groups who left higher-altitude Mendi and Kola areas and settled in the lower eastern valleys of Enga, where they were welcomed by kin (Map 4:1). We estimate that clan sizes at the time were between 60 and 200 residents. The eastern valleys could support a large population; however, in the subsequent generations, numerous conflicts broke out around control of the salt–stone axe trade and other social and political concerns, expelling groups to northern areas that had largely been used as hunting grounds. There they formed the Kopona dialect division (see Map 2 and Map 4:2).

Central Enga and the upper Lagaip (Laiagam area) did not experience the same waves of migration as eastern Enga. Nonetheless, substantial internal population shifts occurred as the tribes of Lyaini and Sakalini living in higher altitudes in the Sirunki area fought large-scale wars to gain land in the lower adjacent Ambum

Table 3 Number of and reasons for migrations of entire tribes or clans reported in tribal histories from the founding generations until the fourth and fifth generations before the present

	Number of migrations	Number of migrant clans	Mean number of clans per migration	Range	Conflict	Social/economic
Into Eastern Enga	12	49	4.0	1–12	2	10
Eastern Enga	10	53	5.3	1–10	7	3
Central Enga	13	59	4.54	2–8	4	9
Upper Lagaip	8	26	3.25	1–7	4	4
Mid-/lower Lagaip	17	37	2.17	1–5	11	6
Kandep	16	21	1.3	1–3	6	10

valley, driving the residents of Pumane and Aiele into the sparsely populated western Kompiam region (Map 4:4). In the lower Ambum valley the tribes of Yanaitini and Yakani expelled Sene-Yokasa to the Sau, Wale and Tarua valleys in a brutal series of wars (Map 4:3). With the Ambum wars, 160 square kilometers of land were taken as twenty-one clans were forced out of the valley and twenty-two clans moved into the vacated land. The expelled groups prospered in the northeast, where they now comprise the Sau Enga dialect group (Map 2).

The upper Lagaip valley also saw major conflicts as tribes inhabiting the higher country moved down into the valleys to profit from the new crop, obtaining rights from in-laws. Major wars are said to have continued for ten to thirty years until the large Kunalini tribe was totally uprooted with the constituent clans fleeing in all directions to establish new residences where they were welcomed by allies or kin (Map 4:5). The victors, the Sambe tribe, took most of the land in the Laiagam area. Despite the dispersal of Kunalini, ties remained and the upper Lagaip became a node for interaction in the development of larger systems of trade, ritual and ceremonial exchange.

West of the Keta river begins the country of the Tayato Enga. There, the oral history portrays quite a different pattern of tribal dispersal and migration both in scale and causes. It no longer tells of large wars that displaced entire tribes but of smaller intra-tribal wars that uprooted entire clans or large subclans with an average of 2.2 clans per migration (Map 4:6). Of the seventeen migrant groups that left their homelands to settle elsewhere, eleven left following conflicts and six left in search of new land; additionally, many extended families moved to join migrant groups. To the south in the Kandep area – a high-altitude, swampy basin – most sweet potato migrations were again smaller, with an average of 1.3 clans per migration. As masters of ritual life, middlemen in the trade with the Huli and Mandi and suppliers for ceremonial exchange, Kandep residents kept themselves well placed on the map of social, religious and economic events.

To give a sense of the dynamics of the post–sweet potato wars and migrations, the following account describes a war in which two brother tribes were ousted around the seventh generation before the present. It portrays the viciousness of some wars of the time, the devastation to the economy, the payment of compensation to allies and the importance of allies for obtaining new residences.

> In those days, warfare was prevalent and it was in one of these wars that the sons of Yoponda and Nenaini became involved ... The war broke out after a quarrel about a stolen boar and a tussle over a piece of land through which one man was building a garden fence ... The war that followed was one of the longest that was ever fought in the area. It went on and on until there was no more food left and all the pig stock was destroyed too. When the war was over, compensation payments still had to be made, but Nenaini and Yoponda had no pigs with which to pay [compensation to their allies] and so they were

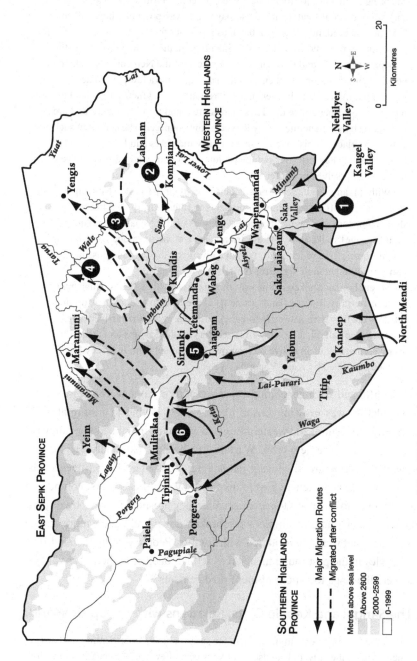

Map 4 Major migrations after the arrival of the sweet potato

faced with another problem besides war. Nevertheless, my grandfather's father's grandfather ... asked the Saka people to hunt and kill some possums and bring them down to Kola to help make his compensation. All that Nenaini and Yoponda could gather for these payments was possums; however, the Saka people brought along pigs, bananas and other foods ...

Among those who came from the Saka region, the leading group was the Sassipakuni people and they came to the rescue of the Nenaini and Yoponda people. Compensation was then paid with possums and a few pigs. When they saw the plight in which the Nenaini and Yoponda found themselves, spokesmen from Sassipakuni said: "These lands are caught up in warfare and are conquered by your enemies. Why do you allow your feet to be caught in such a troubled place as this? We are seeking new members and have much land that is vacant. Pay off your compensation debts and come to make a new home for yourselves in our territory."

Without any hesitation or reluctance on their part, the Nenaini and Yoponda paid off their compensation debts to [their allies] ... After making these compensation payments, representatives of the Nenaini and Yoponda Palu [lineage] spoke thus: "These friends have come to rescue us from this troublesome place, so let us go. We have given you the pigs and possums for compensation and now we leave our territory to you."

When they had spoken in this way, they gave away those lands which made up their territory in Kola [lands named]. These lands made up their original territory but they gave it away before they left Kola. When they arrived here [in the Minyamp valley], they were given territory by the Sassapakuni people and were left there by them to live on their own. (Abridged from R. Lacey [1975: 259–60]; narrated by Kale, Yoponda, Walya)

By the fifth and sixth generations, many groups in Enga were in dire straits. The population was growing in the major valleys owing to in-migration in eastern Enga. In central and western Enga clans moved into the lower valleys to take advantage of the new crop. Warfare had become extremely vicious and destructive in some areas, causing major migrations of eight to fifteen clans. Patterns of trade and exchange were disrupted by significant wars, compelling migrant groups to find ways to reconnect after they prospered in their own areas. Moreover, older stable coalitions were broken down and larger, more fragile ones formed that were often riddled with conflict. People who had lived different lifestyles in the past found themselves settled together in the lower valleys. How were the Enga to get out of these predicaments?

4 The Sangai and Kepele Cults: Relations with the Spirit World

Because the spirit woman made men, the sacred objects [representing her] always helped men, the ugly and handsome alike, so that they would be healthy and good-looking.

(Origin myth for the Sangai bachelors' cult)

The sixth and seventh generations saw the greatest turmoil in precolonial Enga history after the population redistributed over the landscape in order to take advantage of opportunities the new crop offered. However, economic change alone does not restructure a society or build the social and political scaffolding for new institutions. It requires accompanying changes in motivations and values, as well as the resolution of cultural contradictions that inhibit cooperation. Big-men saw the potential of pigs as a currency for social integration that would strengthen their own enterprises and those of their clanspeople. However, the switch to labor-intensive pig production as a central economic activity took considerable cajoling and manipulation from those on top and the positioning of pigs at the center of ceremonial activities.

Intensive sweet potato agriculture accentuated some fundamental contradictions of Enga society that had to be resolved to restore harmonious economic and social cooperation. One contradiction was the principle of initial equal status of all men followed by the challenge to work to become wealthy and influential. Tensions between equality and distinction were heightened with the potential for surplus pig production once the value of surplus pigs and later pearlshells had been socially constructed (Modjeska 1982). A second contradiction in Enga society was the separation of men and women based on menstrual contamination beliefs that was so necessary in times of warfare but that ran contrary to the fundamental interdependence of men and women for production, reproduction and exchange. Finally, most wars were with neighboring clans, though most spouses and wealth for exchanges came from neighbors. War put serious constraints on economic growth and affected individual clan members differentially depending on their ties with opposing clans. New ways to mediate this internal contradiction were sought in order to build more durable, larger coalitions. As was long-standing practice, the Enga turned to ritual to alter values and mediate contradictions. Here we discuss two major initiatives: the Sangai bachelors' cults and the Kepele cults for the ancestors.

4.1 Sangai Bachelors' Cults

Sangai bachelors' cults were developed around the seventh generation in the high country that separates the Ambum/Lai and Lagaip valleys. Former individual rites of seclusion in the forest for young men to promote physical growth and maturity were expanded into communal bachelors' cults. Historical narratives do not tell of the Sangai's origin. It appears to have emerged gradually in a number of places; however, the charter myth is a compelling one: through symbolic group marriage to a spirit woman during secretive cult rites, all bachelors would be transformed into handsome, mature, capable men if they remained faithful to her. The Sangai bonded young men for life and put them firmly in the grips of elders who molded disciplined cohorts for agricultural production, warfare and exchange and determined eligibility for marriage to human women.

The Sangai began with the retreat of the young men to a rudimentary hut in the forest (Schwab and Gibbs 1995). There they remained under the supervision of one or more senior bachelors who presided over ceremonies. Before entering the hut, the youths were cleansed of all impure thoughts and experiences by the painful rite of lying open-eyed under a waterfall. During the four to five days and nights spent in the seclusion of the Sangai hut, the youths were given little to eat or drink and deprived of sleep. By day, they passed their time cleansing their bodies, making wigs and caring for the sacred objects representing the spirit woman: the sweet flag plant (*Acorus calmus*) and/or a bamboo tube filled with liquid representing the blood of the spirit woman (*penge*). "Adultery" with human women damaged the sacred objects, requiring the entire cohort to raise wealth so as to purchase replacements.

In the evening and during the night, the bachelors learned Sangai poetry and magic spells. The longest poem (*sangai titi pingi nemongo*) told of former night journeys to purchase the sacred objects, dangers faced along the way and how the sacred objects made participants rich and famous. The names and accomplishments of wealthy leaders were called out to mold the coalitions of future generations. Only those with keen minds fully mastered the long melodic chants. Sangai poetry did not inculcate military values (Gray 1973; Wiessner and Tumu 1998), only economic and political competencies. Late night was a time for political education. The bachelors fell into brief periods of sleep, awoke, discussed their dreams and composed songs to advise the clan from their visions. Youths attended Sangai ceremonies periodically until elders judged them as mature and marriageable.

The Sangai spread rapidly as surrounding clans sought to keep up with their neighbors (Lacey 1975; Wiessner and Tumu 1998). Elders, who traveled widely, identified other groups whom they perceived as having successful cohorts of youths. Youths then set off on night journeys to secretly bring over the sacred objects together with ritual experts to teach rites and incantations. All Enga cult transmission had a similar nonhierarchical structure; the recipients became the true cult owners, fitting the rites to their local needs and selling them to others (Wiessner and Tumu 1999). The import rituals provided influential leaders with some potential to steer the course of change by subtly setting new ideals. Additional benefits accrued from the spread of the Sangai: the teaching of norms regarding male–female relations facilitated the intergroup marriages on which exchange ties were built.

Communal bachelors' cults appear to have originated in the Sirunki area of central Enga. From there they were adopted by clans of the Lagaip valley and later by those in the upper Ambum valley and central Enga, homogenizing beliefs and practices between people of different valleys. Around the fifth generation, public emergence ceremonies were added to present to the public the future cohort of young men and their prophetic songs composed from dreams. The first in the procession were self-assured older bachelors who were similarly dressed with well-oiled, glistening skin, bodies adorned with ornaments and layers of full-length aprons and heads topped with broad wigs (Figure 6). The last in the line were skinny, awkward novices striving to catch up with their older "brothers." It was not hard to imagine that the spirit woman did indeed play a role in their transformation.

With the appeal of the popular emergence ceremonies, the Sangai spread to easternmost Enga by the third and fourth generations, where it was called Sandalu. Big-men took advantage of the large gatherings that occurred at emergence ceremonies to plan upcoming wealth exchanges once ceremonies were complete. Within the living memory of elders, female suitors in eastern Enga engaged in bawdy, competitive fighting for their Sangai boyfriends, indicating that women's status increased hand in hand with the large exchange systems. This innovation spread widely and amused crowds.

Figure 6 Young men emerging from Sangai ceremony (courtesy of Polly Wiessner, Mulisos, 1985)

4.2 The Kepele Cult

The history of the Kepele cult for the ancestors is shrouded in myth and not easy to unravel, though its political and economic goals and repercussions are clear. The former Kepele cult was held by mobile groups inhabiting higher altitudes in order to gather boys for the Mote initiation; the symbolism in the Mote referred largely to the forest, hunting and gathering. After the movement to the valleys and the shift to sweet potato cultivation, it was transformed into a celebration for the ancestors that tied people to place though many of its foundational elements were maintained. Tribes dispersed by post–sweet potato migrations were drawn together periodically to form larger cooperative political units where young men were inculcated with shared values, emphasis was placed on surplus pig production and exchange ties were forged internally and with the many visitors who attended.

The widely known origin myth for the development of the Kepele had at its center the rocky transition from heavy dependence on forest foods to agriculture:

> Maulu, an agriculturalist from southern Kandep, travelled north into the high country seeking somebody to help him clear a new garden. There he encountered a snakeman, Bipi Molopai, sitting alone in a clearing. Bipi invited him to stay for the night and Maulu accepted, wondering where he would sleep for there was no shelter. As evening fell, Molopai's sons converged on the clearing from all directions, singing and bearing bundles of food from the forest. In a flash they assembled a house from their own bodies, some becoming the walls and others the beams or posts. Bipi hosted Maulu with a lavish meal of forest products and sent his favorite son back with him to clear the garden.
>
> Following the father's demand, Maulu let Bipi Molopai's son sleep alone in the men's house. After three days Maulu's curiosity overcame him and he went to the house at night. There he found a large python encircling the house. The next night he and his clansmen clubbed the rainbow python and put him in the oven pit with hot stones. Bipi's son woke up in the earth oven, crawled out and escaped. The young man was severely wounded on his head. On his way home he took some *take* leaves to bind his wounds and cut a *pai* stick to use as a crutch. He spent many nights along the way on his journey home and each place where he stopped became a Kepele cult site. He arrived at Bipi ceremonial ground which was the origin place of the Kepele cult and rested there. (Peter Yomo of the Sai clan, Mutipa, 1988, and Painda Kaimane of the Wapinyo clan, Longap, 1988)

The original core of the pre–sweet-potato Kepele ritual, which included house building and the Mote boys' initiation, was retained and elaborated as it spread. The process of building the Kepele house formally expressed the relations of different tribal segments to the whole. These were acted out in a drama of house construction where clans or subclans converged on the house site in full ceremonial dress, bringing their own contributions. Each clan or subclan provided one post for the house walls as Molopai's sons did in the Kepele origin myth. The sacred area where the Mote initiation and rites for the ancestors were held was fenced off.

> When it was time to build new houses for the Kepele, each clan was delegated to bring certain materials. Tiangane and Malataini cut *ipiliaka* logs in the high forest, greased them with *mamba* oil and carried them to the ceremonial grounds in a parade. Other Tiangane sub-clans collected posts for the ritual houses and round stones for the earth ovens. Malataini clans usually brought *aepa* [cedar] bark, collected other bush materials and Maliwane provided *lyau* wood and gave the stone axe to cut the wood. They all came to Papyuka singing and dancing in ceremonial attire. Together they built several different houses including one with a tall pinnacle. (Councillor Amu, Sambe Tiangane clan, Papyuka, 1991)

By the seventh generation, sacred objects and rites for the ancestors were added to the Kepele, providing common orientation between eastern and western ancestral cults. Representations of female ancestors included stone mortars, other stones shaped like vaginas or flat round baskets. Images of male ancestors, Yupini, were basketwork figures woven in the image of a man and dressed in ceremonial clothing said to have been introduced in the sixth and seventh generations by a man named Tauni who took his inspiration from the Sepik area to the north. In the seclusion of the cult house, the male and female figures were made to copulate, fed pork fat and laid to rest in tribal land.

On the opening day of the main ceremonies described in eyewitness accounts, all members of the host tribe converged, bringing pigs and other foodstuffs. Guests contributed marsupials and other specialties from their own areas, combining the harvest of the agricultural and hunting economies. The next morning the pigs were clubbed and the pork prepared separately by different procedures for the initiates, adult males, ritual experts and very old men. The large pig kill marked the beginning of the Kepele rites to take place within the enclosed sacred area. During the Mote initiation, boys were symbolically separated from their mothers and the impurities of breast milk, introduced to the secrets of the spirit world, given moral instruction and made to partake of "water of life" so as to promote longevity. Warrior values were not inculcated (Gray 1973; Wiessner and Tumu 1998). The images and rites of the Mote initiation evoked forest life with the bark plaques depicting sun, moon, animals, specific sky people and, above all, representations of the Molopai rainbow python, a symbol of regeneration.

The Kepele of the larger Lagaip tribes incorporated proceedings to combat sicknesses believed to be caused by angry spirits of the dead. The skulls of all recently deceased tribesmen were deposited in a central skull house on the

Kepele site where private rites were held to dampen the harmful agency of ghosts; later the entire lot was banished to the realm of the ancestors through ceremonial cremation. In some Kepele performances there was formal competition at the end of ceremonies as segments of a tribe divided and vied to pull down or burn the cult house, signaling successful completion of the ceremony.

The Kepele drew large crowds; virtually every phase of the Kepele was elaborated into a social event that culminated in the consumption of specially prepared pork (Wiessner 2001). The Kepele offered a rare opportunity for participants and visitors from far and wide to gather, trade, socialize, engage in exchange and arrange marriages in a harmonious, festive atmosphere. The days of joint feasting, dancing, singing, youth initiations and sacred rites united larger groups (Hayden 2014). Such ceremonies reduced internal tensions and promoted collective action at the level of the tribe; peace had to prevail between the two to twelve clans in the often-dispersed tribes in order for Kepele ceremonies to take place. The Kepele had egalitarian appeal: even though ritual experts and big-men invested resources to organize the event, every male had to contribute one pig and only one pig. Kepele celebrations, which placed pork feasts at the center of attention, did much to increase incentives to raise pigs (Wiessner 2001).

The Kepele cult spread widely. Unlike other Enga cults, it formed an interconnected ritual network described as a rainbow python with its head in Kandep and its tail in the Porgera valley (Gibbs 1978) (Map 5). We documented fifty-five sites; no doubt there were more. Each tribe recognized the unifying Kepele origin tradition, though each also had a legitimizing origin tradition for their own Kepele. Ritual experts from other sites were invited to co-preside in rites, providing some unity to the network. Visitors from other tribes could travel freely, for it was forbidden for enemies to attack people traveling to and from Kepele performances. Aside from having local influence, the Kepele did much to lay down standard ideas, practices and the infrastructure for tribal and intertribal relations, giving some unity to western Enga.

In summary, the response to the turmoil generated by the reassortment of groups following the arrival of the sweet potato was the emergence of numerous cults to alter motivations and values, to address the long-standing contradictions in Enga culture and to help build new infrastructures for more complex economic and political institutions. The Sangai and Kepele are just two examples. Sangai bachelors' cults laid down a clear age structure of authority, underwrote equality, gave young men an assured path to marriage and relief from contamination fears that inhibited male–female cooperation. The Sangai bonded the cohorts that would form the cooperative economic and political protagonists of the future. The Kepele standardized ideas and values throughout western Enga, reducing conflict between groups oriented toward hunting and those relying

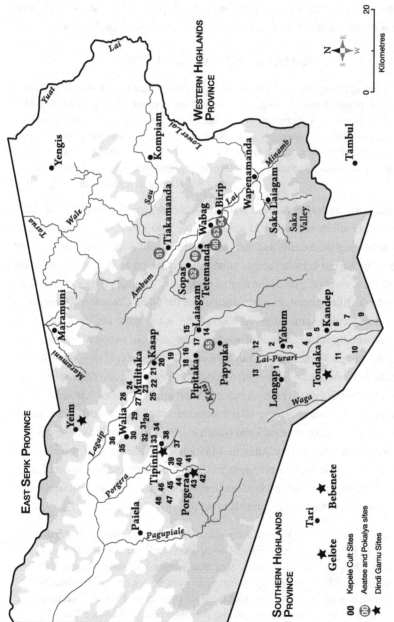

Map 5 Kepele, Aetee and Pokalya ritual sites

largely on agriculture. It formed larger cooperative economic and political groups, laid down scaffolding for economic ties within and between tribes, and valued pigs as a common currency for exchange. While the snake of Kepele was spreading throughout western Enga, developments in eastern and central Enga were taking different courses for addressing similar challenges.

5 The Great Ceremonial Wars

> The underlying purpose of these Yanda Andake, Great Ceremonial Wars, was to bring people together – they were formal and ceremonial. They were fought to show the numerical strength and solidarity of a tribe and the physical build and wealth of the warriors. Figuratively, it is said that in the wars, they exposed themselves to the sun. The Great Wars were events for socializing. After getting to know each other, they would kill many pigs and hold feasts and exchanges.
>
> (Depoane, Timali clan, Lenge, 1987)

The wars and migrations of the sixth and seventh generations in central Enga forged larger alliances in order to acquire fertile land in the Ambum valley. Such large-scale wars were costly and their aftermaths chaotic. Once land was obtained, conflicts broke out between allies, young men were eager to keep fighting, and migrations severely disrupted the map of trade and exchange (Wiessner and Tumu 1998). In the fifth generation, a new institution, the Great Ceremonial Wars (Great Wars), spectacular, semi-ritualized tournament wars, grew out of the desire to preserve some positive aspects of warfare – larger-scale cooperation, display of strength, stronger leadership and subsequent exchanges with allies – while eliminating the most damaging ones – unbridled death, disruption and destruction. They were fought repeatedly over generations in what might be called "episodes" every eight to twenty years, placing heavy demands on food production to sustain participants for weeks or months and wealth to supply the Great War compensatory exchanges. As described by Ambone Mati who witnessed two of the last Great Wars, these spectacular events rewove former trade routes, created new routes into areas where migrants had resettled and forged the social and political scaffolding that allowed economic developments to unfold.

> The Great Wars were planned and planted like a garden for the exchanges that would follow. They were arranged when goods and valuables were plentiful and when there were so many pigs that women complained about their workloads. Everybody knew what they were in for, how compensation would be paid for deaths, and what the results would be. They were designed to open up new areas, further existing exchange relations, foster tribal unity, and provide a competitive, but structured environment in which young men could strive for leadership. These qualities of the Great Wars made them differ from conventional wars. The latter disrupted relationships of trade and exchange, causing turmoil and sometimes damage that could not be repaired.

The distributions of wealth that took place after the Great Wars brought trade goods from outlying areas into the Wabag area on the trade paths initially established by the salt trade. (Ambone Mati, Nemani clan, Kopen, 1988)

5.1 Protagonists in the Great Wars

Four Great Wars were fought, building dense ties over four valley systems: the Lai, Lagaip, Ambum and Sau (Map 6). The first was the Yanaitini–Monaini Great War that began around the sixth generation or earlier (Map 6:3). As the legend goes, Yanaitini found that the sweet potato grew well at Tetemanda and subsequently moved there, away from his brother tribe the Itokone, to be in a better position to channel the salt–stone axe trade. Apparently Monaini, a large tribe of the Lagaip, felt that its position in the trade was threatened by the move and "stole Yanaitini's sweet potato" in response. The conflict was remembered in a song sung during the Yanaitini–Monaini Great War: "Being hungry, took out a Sanda (Yanaitini's) sweet potato. You never stop crying over the sweet potato."

Pisoto Pisini, the oldest member of the Yanaitini tribe, remembered participating in the last episode of this Great War between 1915 and 1920 when he was in his teens. He was too young to understand the political context of the war, but he recalled his stay of approximately six months with hosting families in the Sambe tribe near Laiagam, the excitement of battles, their glamour and spectacle, and the courtship of parties at night. This Great War ended early in the twentieth century.

The second Great War was the Lyaini-Sakalini versus the Pumane-Aiele, which had roots in the Ambum valley wars of the sixth and seventh generations when the former drove the latter to the upper Sau area. We could not determine from historical narratives if earlier episodes were more conventional wars; however, by the fourth generation it had become a true tournament war. Because Pumane-Aiele clans were widely dispersed, participants came from a vast area to the northeast (Map 6:1). The last episode of this Great War was fought in the early twentieth century for reasons discussed later.

The third Great War was the Sene-Yokasa versus the Yakani, a conflict that also had its roots in the Ambum wars. Sene and Yokasa prospered in their new area, the Sau valley, and so were eager to place themselves back on the map of trade and exchange. Yakane had an interest in building exchange ties to gain access to the large pig herds their opponents could raise in their fertile new areas of residence (Map 6:4). We were able to determine that two and most likely three episodes of this Great War were fought in the fourth generation. Historical narratives describing the last war between the Sene-Yokasa and the Yakane are

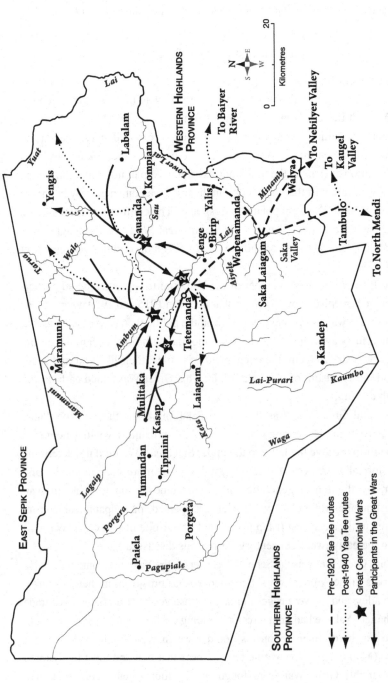

Map 6 Location of the Great Wars in relation to the Tee cycle 1. Lyaini-Sakalini versus Pumane-Aiele; 2. Itapuni-Awaini versus Malipini-Potealini; 3. Monaini versus Yanaitini; 4. Yakani versus Sene-Yokasa

detailed, although nobody who fought in it was still alive at the time of our work. The designated battlefield was initially in the upper Sau valley, although later episodes were fought at Wakumale near the confluence of the Ambum and Lai rivers. The last episode was fought in the early twentieth century (see Sections 8 and 10).

The fourth Great War, between the Malipini-Potealini and the Itapuni Awaini, was sparked by an amusing "peeping Tom" incident that stirred up antagonisms between neighbors who had been competitors for generations in the upper Lai valley (Map 6:2). Ambone Mati of the Itapuni tribe told us that one and probably several episodes were fought in the fourth to fifth generations and could recall five fought in his father's lifetime and two fought in his lifetime. The last was fought in the late 1930s or early 1940s. Earlier episodes were hosted by clans in the upper Lai and recent ones by clans at the Lai–Ambum confluence.

5.2 The Course of the Great Wars

Here we will give a general description of the Great Wars, although they certainly varied over time and space (Wiessner and Tumu 1998). No doubt the earlier episodes began with less structured fighting and compensatory exchanges, testing out the strength of opponents, and became more formalized in later generations as exchange networks grew. Unfortunately, oral records are insufficient to trace such developments, so we must rely on testimonies of elder informants who fought in the wars, their fathers or their grandfathers.

The Great Wars involved not just single clans and their allies but all constituent clans of a tribe or two brother tribes and their allies. All conventional warfare within these tribes had to be terminated to unify for the Great Wars. When a Great War was to be fought, "the owners of the fight" asked intermediary tribes to host them. For the duration of the Great War, warriors lived with hosting clans and fought within a designated locale, so no land was won or lost. The hosting clans provided food, water, housing and frontline warriors, forging close personal relationships between hosts, owners of the fight and allies. Hosts had to intensify staple production to feed the warriors for weeks or months, though some warriors initially brought supplies. It is said that even some spectators killed pigs. Sweet potatoes cannot be stored for long, so additional gardens had to be cleared and planted to ripen in time to supply the war. In turn, the owners of the fight had to raise pigs for the Great War exchanges; large pigs took five to six years to raise when well fed with sweet potato. Breaks were called so that men and women could tend to their pigs and gardens. Workloads of both men and women were greatly increased, and the value of pigs also rose. In the earlier Great Wars, cassowaries and different species of possums were hunted so as to provision the feasts and exchanges:

> During the postwar exchanges, many cassowaries were also given for Sakatawane was renowned for its ability to capture cassowaries. Along my ridge, one would find many ponds made to water cassowaries brought for the wealth distribution. There is also a stretch of Kamaniwane land where pools can still be found and at Lakui there are three such ponds. We would give not only cassowaries but all kinds of marsupials (possums). (Pyakole Pyakena, Malyee clan, Lai–Ambum ridge, 1988)

Each clan and household enjoyed considerable autonomy over the extent of their participation, selecting the households who would host them, usually those with kinship ties. Warriors lived in the houses of their hosts or in men's houses built specially for the occasion. Each night warriors ate together with hosts and allies, rehashed the battle, and engaged in courtship parties with young women from the hosting and allied clans. Strong bonds were formed during these weeks of co-residence that turned to kinship relations when marriages resulted from nightly courtship parties.

> Look, the warriors stayed and spent the nights in the houses of Yanaitini clans or in Malipini and Potealini houses that were near the battlefront . . . they did not go home after a day's fight; they only returned when the Great War was over. When they first arrived, they would bring food for a few days, but after that people of the hosting clans fed them. It was a great occasion – many of the girls from surrounding communities would come and entertain us . . . All nights were social nights; we had lots of fun with the girls. We courted them by night and went to fight during the day. It was exciting and fun. Of course, that meant that some of us would eventually end up marrying them. (Yopo Yakena, Kamaniwane clan, 1987)

The Great Wars reversed the usual strict separation of men and women during warfare and contradictions between men's and women's roles in war. By day, women sang and danced along the sidelines of the battlefield, cheering on the warriors, and by night, they engaged in courtship parties.

The Great Wars were organized and led by big-men called *watenge* – organizers, orators and showmen who had the political ties and savvy to coordinate their followers for battles and subsequent distributions of wealth. *Watenge* had to have good knowledge of military strategy but did not need to be outstanding warriors; it was strictly taboo to kill *watenge* during the Great Wars because they were the ones who would organize exchanges. However, attempts were made to humiliate them by briefly capturing them and pluck-ing the plumes from their headdresses. There was at least one *watenge* from each participant clan, though some rose to extraordinary prominence. Planning and mobilization of personnel and resources took weeks in order to brew a Great War:

> People would hold a traditional dance together with allied forces, hosts, and enemies called the *yanda andaka ia minao mali lyingi*, the dance for breeding the Great War. Everybody dressed in such a way as to indicate his intentions, songs of provocation and rivalry were exchanged, and *watenge* from both sides made speeches. They boasted of the bravery of their warriors and how well their host would look after them, and they mocked the enemy for how little they had given away in the exchanges after the last episode [years earlier]. The tension mounted between the two sides but the actual war did not start there. First the warriors would go to the land of the host clans and spend days on end talking about the upcoming event. (Yopo Yakena, Kaimaniwane clan, Kaeyape, 1987)

On the appointed day, hundreds of warriors converged on the battlefield for the opening ceremonies adorned in full ceremonial attire; those who did not own these items borrowed them in exchange for gifts, seeking to dress like other members of their clan in order to express unity (Figure 7). While spectators from near and far gathered to watch, fight leaders met, greeted one another, exchanged boasting songs, embraced or exchanged axes, sang provocative challenges, and called a beginning to the battle.

Figure 7 Traditional dance, *sing-sing*, held during the Great Wars, Tee cycle and other ceremonial events (courtesy of Don Jeffers, mid-Lai, 1960s)

The actual fighting followed the procedures of conventional wars, but because ambushes and raids were forbidden, the death toll was low. Four to five warriors were killed in more recent episodes. Victims were mourned as men who had died for a good cause, but deaths were not avenged because the Great Wars were said to be wars without anger. After weeks or months of intermittent battles, leaders agreed to call a formal end to the Great War by lining up weapons and casting them into the river. Mature men looked forward to the exchanges that would follow when the bonds engendered during the Great War would result in partnerships of trade and exchange. Young men lamented the end of the excitement, returning home crying "Yandao" as if mourning the end of the war:

> The Great Wars were like a game for young people that everybody enjoyed playing ... On our way home, we wiped the tears from our eyes saying, "the days in which we entertained ourselves in the Great War are gone now and it will be a sad day through and through." With these words we cried as we walked slowly home. (Waingia Lyambi, Malipini Sakatawane clan, Sopas, 1988)

5.3 Great War Exchanges

After the battles had ended, feasts and wealth exchanges were held as the owners of the fight paid the hosts for their hospitality. These compensatory exchanges would continue for two to four years. During the weeks or months of the war, close relationships that had formed between the hosts and hosted warriors established exchange partnerships. These exchanges conformed to reparations paid to allies lost in conventional wars except that they were much larger and more elaborate:

1. *Endaki kamungi* (fetching water): initiatory gifts of cooked pork, marsupial meat, cassowaries, goods and valuables were given to the owners of the fight by the hosts in a feast held shortly after the formal end to battle. The name refers to the fact that the hosts had fetched water for the owners of the fight, provided for them during the fighting, fought with them as allies, and now were expecting returns.
2. *Kepa singi and akali buingi*. Reparations were paid for all allied men killed by the hosting clans. Enemy deaths were not compensated; any exchanges between the opponents were strictly forbidden.
3. *Yanda andake kepa singi*. An extraordinary large payment of raw, butchered pork supplemented by marsupial meat was distributed to the host clans by the owners of the fight. Families from the hosting clans attended the clan festivals of the individual men they had hosted to receive their due.

4. *Akaipu tee.* Initiatory gifts for the final payments given by the hosts to the owners of the fight composed of cooked pork, goods and valuables.
5. *Lome nyingi.* This large final payment included live pigs, cassowaries, marsupials, goods and valuables given by the owners of the fight to the hosts. *Lome nyingi* means to build a stronghold, implying that the host had opened their stronghold to the owners of the fight.

In the last Great War of the late 1930s, more than twenty participant clans killed some 1,000 to 2,000 pigs on one day. Hosts and allies awoke at dawn and traveled from clan to clan, over hill and dale, collecting pork from families they had hosted. The following describes the *yanda andake kepa singi* owners of the fight gave to their hosts:

> The Great War pig kill would begin on the land of Potealini Kombatao and Wambili clans in the upper Lai valley. It began very early, before daybreak. Then at daybreak the Kombatao clan killed their pigs. The Sakatawane clan at Sopas killed pigs about the time that we usually open house doors in the morning. The pork was then brought to one ceremonial ground after another ... There was so much pork that they had to give away the meat uncooked. Additional meat was left on the sides of pork so that those who received it could cut it off, cook it and eat it on their way back before they passed the sides of pork on to people further down the Lai.
>
> In the meantime, Yanaitini men [the hosts] got ready to attend these festivals putting on their wigs of human hair, chest plates, and on top of their wigs, woven cassowary headdresses. Dressed in this way, they went to the ceremonial grounds, sat down and waited for men from the owners of the fight to bring in the pork and distribute it. The donors entered, bringing some steamed sides of pork and many that were raw ... All of the men from hosting or assisting in Yanaitini clans received sides of pork, and in turn they gave them to men in the Kalia clan and clans who sent them eastward.
>
> In the Ambum valley, the Kamaniwane clan killed pigs at sunrise. When the sun was just above the horizon, the men from Potealini at Tiakamanda killed pigs. In the middle of the day, men from the Kombane, Angalaene and Wailuni clans killed pigs, and just after midday, men from the Itapu area killed theirs. All this was done in one day.
>
> During these festivals, Yanaitini men who had hosted warriors went around from ceremonial ground to ceremonial ground in full attire to receive sides of pork and other portions of meat. Many open fires could be seen along the paths where people stopped to roast pork. In the evening they went straight to bed not feeling hungry at all. (Yopo Yakena, Kamaniwane clan, Kaeyape, 1987)

The Great War protocols reduced internal contradictions in Enga society. During the Great Wars peace had to be made between all participant groups on both sides, alleviating tension between neighboring clans. The strict separation of men and women during warfare was relaxed. Importantly, the contradiction between principles of equality versus achieved hierarchy was skillfully managed. *Watenge*, Great War leaders, were not only chosen internally but also by the enemy who challenged certain leaders on the other side to present themselves during battle. Between Great Wars, they were big-men in their own clans. Unlike the average big-man of the time, whose power base was seated in his fellow clansmen, the status of Great War leader required maternal and affinal ties with leading families of hosting and allied groups through which they could wield regional influence. The public appreciated the connections and capacities of Great War leaders for organization, coordination, regional ties and showmanship.

The Great Wars mitigated emerging social inequalities by offering something for everybody appropriate to gender and age: entertainment, bonding, display and exchange ties for all men and women, with different phases and activities appealing to different age groups. Significant individual autonomy existed; warriors chose the families who would host them and with whom they would form exchange ties. Wealth was not pooled in the hands of big-men, so all participants had agency. While everybody stood to gain, those in leadership positions who got the big picture of how the Great Wars worked had the knowledge to play events to their own advantage more than did the average participant. Their widespread popularity and benefits dampened tensions between equality and hierarchy and facilitated growth. The Great Wars transformed the economy from one based largely on household production to one based on surplus production to fund these great events with political as well as economic goals. However, one weak point would have been fatal had other developments not occurred: the fact that they were financed by household production (Strathern 1969). As the Great Wars grew, leaders sought new economic solutions.

6 The Tee Ceremonial Exchange Cycle

> The Tee flows on a path no bigger than a single strand of a spider's web. All care must be taken not to break it.

While impressive efforts were taking place in western and central Enga to readjust society and economy after the arrival of the sweet potato, much quieter developments were occurring in the east: the birth of the Tee Ceremonial Exchange Cycle (Tee Cycle). The early Tee Cycle, also called the Yae Tee, introduced a new system of finance that was to become a game-changer for the Enga economy. It drew on former exchange traditions in Enga society; this

Figure 8 Bridewealth with pigs and pearlshells (courtesy of Ian Walsh, Kompiam area, 1975)

section will trace its development, though the ramifications of this new system will become apparent only in later sections.

Tee exchange, called *tee pingi* in Enga – to ask for – and *moka* in the Melpa and Pidgin languages, involved the ceremonial exchange of pigs, goods, food and valuables; it was the social and political glue of Enga.[1] *Tee pingi* differs from trade (*aloa pingi*) that was an economic transaction used to acquire goods and valuables, while *tee* exchange was carried out in public and designed to build social and political connections by circulating wealth. Many forms of *tee* exchange appear to have deep roots in Enga culture; all forms of *tee* involved delayed returns. Bridewealth exchanges, *enda yole maingi*, initiated lifelong gift exchanges between extended families in different clans with lineage and other clan members of the groom contributing; some exchange pigs were the given by the bride's family (Figure 8). Bridewealth compensated for the transfer of the woman's labor and childbearing potential to her husband's clan.

A number of smaller *tee* exchanges between families in different clans developed out of marriage. Child growth payments, *wane kenge singi*, were given by a husband's lineage to his wife's kin to recognize her efforts in bearing and raising their children; child injury payments, *beta pingi*, were given by a husband's lineage to his wife's kin for injury in childhood or adulthood. *Laita*

---

[1] *Tee* is pronounced as "tay," not "tea."

pingi involved the transfer of larger amounts of wealth to the mother's kin after funeral proceedings were complete. These smaller exchanges were often used as building blocks to assemble wealth for larger exchanges such as warfare compensation and the Tee Cycle.

6.1 The Origin of the Tee Cycle

The origin of the Tee Cycle is told in legends couched in symbolic speech. Only after years of research have we been able put together a picture of its beginnings and diffusion. The Tee Cycle developed after the arrival of the sweet potato when groups from Tambul (Kakoli) and Mendi (Mandi) areas migrated down into the Saka valley (Map 4). These groups had strong ties to the east and south, threatening Saka Yambatane's control of the salt–axe stone trade alliance between Yanuni of Tambul, Yambatane in the Saka valley, Itokone of the mid-Lai and Yanaitini of Tetemanda, central Enga (Map 6 and Map 7). As the legend goes, Yambatane's grandson Kitalini, who had been in seclusion in the forest after his brothers died of *yama* sickness, took action to keep control of the trade (Wiessner and Tumu 1998):

> One day when Kitalini was a handsome young bachelor, he went to a sing-sing at Alumanda where young women from all over the area came to dance beside him. Lovestruck, three beautiful women, from Melyoposini, Yandamani and Yandamani Yanana, followed Kitalini to his house and wanted to marry him. He showed them that he had no pigs, gardens or regular house and no brothers to help him with bridewealth. He asked them to go home and wait for him. While the women waited anxiously without eating or sleeping, he sent out messages along the Kunja, Sambe, Walepa, Sambaka and Ome trade routes saying, "If people are supposed to help and give, then do so for I need pigs now." People arrived with pigs from all directions and gave them to Kitalini. By the end of four days Kitalini had enough pigs to make a generous bridewealth payment for each woman, keeping the rest to thank the people who had helped him. The parents of the brides gave Kitalini one pig in exchange for each pig he had given.
>
> Kitalini then sent messages back down the Walepa, Kunja, Sambe, Sambaka and Ome routes that he was going to hold a *tee* distribution to pay back those who had helped him. People from all directions gathered on the Alumanda ceremonial grounds. Kitalini lined up the pigs and gave them out, taking pigs that had come along the Sambe route and giving them to people along the Kunja route, and so on. Over the years the exchange between the descendants of Kitalini continued at the Alumanda ceremonial grounds. (Saiyakali Patao Yaki, Yana clan, Saka Laiagam, 1987)

Kitalini's innovation is also mentioned in the history of the neighboring Itokone tribe, giving it more credibility and detail:

In the past there lived a man named Itokone. He fathered Mupa, Nenae, Lanjetakini, Lundopa and Tandaka and then had two more children, Keoyakini and Napukini. Mupa had pigs, but Nenae did not. At Lamandaimanda [middle Lai Valley], the sons of Itokone set out *mena limando* pig stakes. Nenae had no pigs, but he set out *mena kii* stakes on the ceremonial grounds to indicate his planned distribution. Their mother, Itokone's wife from Kaekini, came that morning, checked the line and asked questions about the stakes. Somebody told her that they belonged to the sons of Itokone and that one row belonged to each of his sons.

One line was longer than the other, which prompted her to ask, "Whose stakes are these?"

"They belong to Nenae," she was told.

"Why do you put up a row of pig stakes when you have no pigs in your house?"

He replied, "I am not like my brother Mupa who only breeds pigs . . . You see, I go up there [to the Saka valley and Tambul] and chase down the pigs. That is how I am going to get my pigs. I am not so simple."

So what Nenae and his brothers did was to slaughter pigs and bring sides of pork to the Saka valley. That was called the *saandi pingi* [initiatory gifts]. They did not do it directly, but through the Aluni Kepa clan. They also gave sides of pork to the Waiminakuni clan who in turn gave them to Yambatane. Yambatane took the sides of pork and went to Kuiamanda in Kola [Tambul] . . . In that place, the Tee Cycle was launched. Yambatane then brought the Tee to the Saka valley, took pigs from it and gave them to Waiminakuni, Kepa and Maitepa clans of Aluni. They then gave pigs to Itokone, and the Tee Cycle came to rest at Tilyaposa. Itokone then held their Tee festival and gave pigs to Yakani Timali and so the Tee went up to Lenge. Itokone also gave pigs directly to the Yanaitini Kia clan at Tetemanda. That is how the Tee Cycle was performed in the early stages.

In those days, only the clans I mentioned participated in the Tee and that was the situation for some time. Later, as people in the area saw and heard about the Tee, they began to take part. All others learned from these people and then they joined. That is how the Tee Cycle expanded to other regions. (Palane Yakenalu, Nenae clan, 1987)

The Kitalini legend describes a brilliant economic innovation. In earlier times, people received some wealth to help with payments from immediate relatives only. To increase the wealth that could be assembled in one place at one time, Kitalini, who represents the Yambatane tribe, concatenated former partnerships along the trade routes to construct chains of finance. Wealth was called in from partners several links down the chains, increasing the amount of wealth that arrived at one place and one time by eliciting finance on credit from people who were beyond the usual bounds of kinship reckoning. Tee Cycle exchange partially decoupled economics from kinship and the accompanying protocols and etiquette.

By maximizing the wealth arriving in one place at one time, recipients gained financial clout to engage in political enterprises without having to feed large herds of pigs in their own houses. Wealth was distributed on the ceremonial grounds in public so people could witness who contributed and who was to be paid back. Prior to this time, wealth had been distributed more privately at men's houses. Wealth received in Tee Cycle distributions was often given on the spot to others to expand trade alliances, contract strategic marriages, extend alliances or provide generous compensation for men lost in battle, or pay other debts.

6.2 Structure of the Tee Cycle

By the fourth generation, the Tee Cycle had developed into a three-phase cycle (Meggitt 1972, 1974; Wiessner and Tumu 1998): (1) *saandi pingi*, initiatory gifts; (2) *mena tee pingi*, the distribution of live pigs and pearlshells; and (3) *mena yae pingi*, the slaughtering of half of the pigs received for the distribution of cooked pork (Figure 9). Ideally, a Tee Cycle was to be completed in four years, though some cycles took longer as politics grew more complex. If the cycle started in the east, the *saandi pingi* moved from east to west, *the mena tee pingi* from west to east and the *mena yae pingi* from east to west. The next cycle would move in the opposite direction, starting in the west.

Saandi pingi involved giving initiatory gifts of piglets, possums, small packages of salt, shells, net bags and aprons, tree oil and plumes to exchange partners to request main gifts that were of greater value. Giving *saandi* gifts to begin a Tee Cycle was usually advocated by clan leaders, although it was done privately by individual families. In-laws who had promised to give smaller payments for child growth or injury might be requested to time their payments to help with initiatory gifts. The underlying idea was to convert gifts of lower value into those of higher value by using them as initiatory gifts that would receive greater returns during the *mena tee pingi* phase of the cycle.

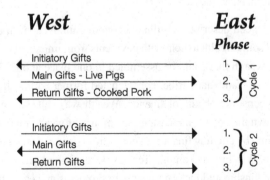

Figure 9 Schematic diagram of an ideal Tee cycle

If a Tee Cycle started in the east at Tambul, all initiatory gifts were given to partners to the west. After acceptance of initiatory gifts, the recipients raised and assembled pigs for the giving of live pigs. The big-men who were Tee organizers would have to travel the entire length of Tee Cycle routes from Tambul to Tetemanda to Kompiam to organize the main phase, *mena tee pingi*. This phase involved the giving of the main gifts of live pigs, pearlshells, stone axes, cassowary and large packages of salt to those who had given initiatory gifts. If the initiatory gifts had moved from east to west, then the *mena tee pingi* would start in the west and move east. Each clan on the Tee Cycle route held a public festival and distribution on its own ceremonial ground, giving to partners' clans living to the east of them. Warfare had to cease between the clans for the Tee to flow. This phase took half a year or longer until all clans had held their distributions. Clan distributions of live pigs and valuables in the *mena tee pingi* were impressive and in more recent generations were attended by some 2,000 to 3,000 people, many from different clans and tribes. The highlight of the *mena tee pingi* was the counting of pigs when big-men in full ceremonial regalia danced down their lines of pigs.

The final phase of a Tee Cycle was the *mena yae pingi* when approximately half of the pigs were slaughtered and the meat distributed to those who had given live pigs as well as to others. When this final phase developed is uncertain. Possibly it was adopted for regulation as the Tee grew and the numbers of pigs to care for beyond the short term became unsustainable (Rappaport 1968). Relieved of the competition, it was a festive event. Meat was kept cool in special houses as it traveled, but still some of the meat rotted, was fed to the dogs or was thrown into the river. While the *mena tee pingi* pushed pig production to the limits, the *mena yae pingi* reduced pig herds to a more manageable size in order to prepare for the next cycle.

6.3 Participation in the Tee Cycle

Any family could participate in the Tee Cycle; the role of big-men was to coordinate clan members to bring in all the wealth obtained from individual Tee chains at one time and distribute it on the clan's ceremonial ground so as to enhance clan status with an impressive show of wealth. Clan meetings were held to discuss timing of the clan's Tee festival and the intentions of families who then planted stakes on the ceremonial grounds to indicate the number of pigs they would distribute. Although Tee Cycle distributions were clan-wide events, wealth was not pooled; participant families gave away their pigs to families of their choice and received returns for their individual investments.

The Tee Cycle was built up from personal ties. Each family had its own Tee partners in other clans – usually related through female kin. An individual or family gave out wealth to their partners and relatives on the clan's ceremonial ground at the same time other clan members did, but nobody had any say over a family's economic transactions. Men distributed the family's pigs, though all transactions were agreed upon by men and women in the privacy of their households (Kyakas and Wiessner 1992). The more wealth a family could give out, the more prestige they gained. The total wealth given out by the clan as a whole was not as important as individual contributions. Individual acheivements were counted; clan totals were not.

Tee Cycle partnerships were organized into chains of partners that could bring wealth from a broad catchment area. These partnerships between men were called *kaita miningi* – holders of the way – and were considered among a person's most valuable relationships. Such Tee partners were referred to as "my best pandanus palm," "my favorite possum tree" or "my *tee* bridge." Enga took great care to not break fragile Tee alliances by diverting wealth or neglecting old partners when new opportunities arose, as expressed in the saying "Don't put out the fire when you see the sun." Tee partners were organized into chains that crossed clan boundaries; initially these chains are said to have clung to the trade route from Tambul to Tetemanda and the trade routes down into the lower Lai (Map 7).

Only one other economic system in the PNG highlands involves a similar principle of concatenating partnerships to tap into the wealth of distant or nonkin in order to finance large distributions of wealth: the Moka of the Western Highlands well described in the work of Strathern (1969, 1971). Because the Moka appears to have developed out of war compensation payments to enemy rather than efforts to control trade routes, it had a different structure than the Enga Tee Cycle: (1) the chains of finance were much longer in the Enga Tee to secure relations along trade routes; (2) although there was competition in the Tee Cycle to do well by giving more than others, the locus of competition was not between donors and recipients as it was in the Moka; returns in the Tee did not involve an increment. Neither individuals nor clans in the Enga Tee tried to outdo others by giving back more than they received they did in the Moka. Finally, Moka payments, like in the war reparations, were given largely by persons in one clan to partners in the opposing clan, whereas those in the Enga Tee were distributed to recipients in several clans.

For two to three generations after the Tee Cycle was initiated, it was performed on a small scale. Historical traditions indicate that the most successful participants distributed no more than five to ten pigs in one clan festival and that the number of clans involved was limited to ten to twenty. The network clung to clans along trade routes and did not attract much attention (Wiessner and Tumu 1998).

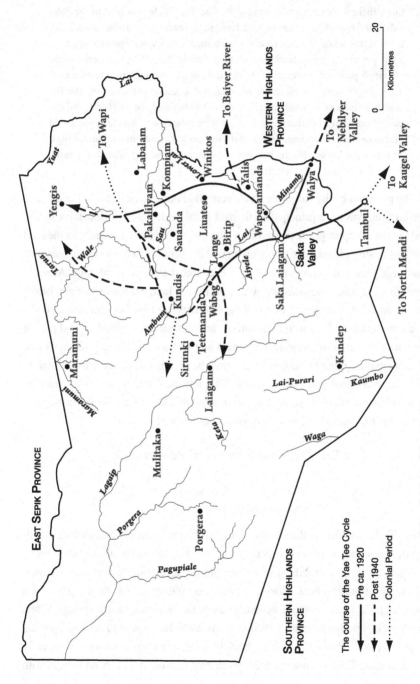

Map 7 Map of Tee cycle routes by chronological stages of development

EAST SEPIK PROVINCE

WESTERN HIGHLANDS PROVINCE

SOUTHERN HIGHLANDS PROVINCE

To Wapi

To Baiyer River

To Nebilyer Valley

To Kaugel Valley

To North Mendi

Labalam
Kompiam
Winikos
Yalis
Wapenamanda
Walya
Pakalilyam
Sau
Sauanda
Liuates
Birip
Lenge
Aiyele
Saka Laiagam
Saka Valley
Tambul
Yengis
Wabag
Tetemanda
Sirunki
Kundis
Laiagam
Kandep
Maramuni
Mulitaka
Lai-Purari
Kaumbo
Porgera
Pagupiale

Lai
Yuet
Lower Lai
Minamb
Wale
Ambum
Maramuni
Tarua
Keta
Lagaip
Porgera
Waga

Kilometres
0   20

The course of the Yae Tee Cycle
Pre ca. 1920
Post 1940
Colonial Period

In the past around the fifth generation, only a few people were involved in the Tee Cycle; only a few promoted the Tee and actually took part in it. In those times there were many who were poor. The Tee Cycle was held in the Saka valley and branched off through the Kungu, Sambaka and Sambe routes . . . In those times when the Tee routes I have mentioned were opening up, only a few people were involved. For instance, here in Birip there were only a few who took part in the Tee; all of the rest did not have enough pigs to take part. They simply were not interested in doing so. Therefore, in those times the Tee was done on a very small scale. That is not to say that the Tee Cycle did not cover a large area but that not many pigs were given away. Most people would give away one or two pigs only, and if a person gave away more than ten pigs, he was regarded as a big-man. It was only later that the Tee expanded greatly. (Apakasa, Depe Lyala clan, Birip, 1990)

The potential of the early Tee Cycle remained unrealized because the average person, who was not a principal participant in the trade, had little incentive to join and lacked the appropriate ties to do so. Not everybody was interested in the hard work of raising pigs to participate given that the economy of average households was largely geared to meet household needs rather than political ones. Allies in warfare were often compensated with a portion of land gained in war and bride-wealth payments composed of a few pigs for feasting together with trade goods. The few pigs raised for wedding, cult or funeral festivals derived a good part of their sustenance from foraging. Only men and women with broader designs saw the potential of pigs as a currency that could be intensively raised and invested to promote individual and clan interests. This left the Enga with a powerful new economic system with limited need, a situation that was to change as the population grew, the land filled, and ceremonial exchange expanded.

7 Conflict Resolution and Peacemaking

> You live long if you plan the death of a pig,
> but not if you plan the death of a person.

It is difficult to understand economic developments without a thorough understanding of institutions to settle conflicts and restore balance. After all, the majority of conflicts, whether interindividual or intergroup, have some economic underpinnings, and if not resolved, economic initiatives will be stifled. As the population grew and the complexity of economic systems increased, what principles and practices of traditional Enga justice systems could be evoked to resolve conflicts at larger scales? This section will address the question of justice systems in the early generations of Enga history and their development through time, hand in hand with the economy.

7.1 Internal Disputes

Disputes and infractions within Enga clans in the past often led to demands for compensation or initial dyadic retaliation followed by material compensation. The focus of compensation was restorative, making up for damages or harm done to the victim, rather than sanctioning. This principle was and still is applied at different levels from individual to intergroup disputes (Wiessner 2019). Kipuli Petakin, a leader from Irelya village, outlined past practice for interindividual disputes:

> I was told of how disputes were settled before the white men came, disputes around landownership and clearance, the ownership of pandanus trees, the abduction of girls and women, theft, particularly the theft of pigs, murder and insufficient goods for compensation. There were no formalities in the settlement of conflicts. Within the clan, the disputing parties told their friends and leaders about the nature of the problem. Then the disputing parties were called to appear at the ceremonial ground before several leaders and the other members of the community ... After both parties had spoken, the matter was left to the leaders for a decision ... The rest of the speakers either supported them or expressed their own opinions regarding the issue and eventually came to an agreement. After giving their reasons for their opinions, they suggested a solution ...
>
> If the decision seemed fair, the owner of the pig who had destroyed a garden would agree to compensate. However, if the amount awarded was too high, the defendant could reject the decision and was supported by the public. Things like pigs, possum tails, beads, woven cassowary and birds of paradise feathers were given in compensation. Leaders would sometimes give either of the parties an item of value for their reparations. (Kipuli Petakin, Apulini clan, Irelya, 1996)

7.2 Intergroup Conflicts

At the intergroup level in earlier generations, compensation was used to repair ties with allies for men lost in battle but not for enemy losses to reestablish peace:

> A long time ago much pork was given to the clans of allies killed in a war, but only one or two pigs were killed to compensate the enemy clan. They were usually given by people closely related to the victim. But as I said earlier, even if the victim in the enemy clan had relatives on the other side, not many pigs were killed to pay reparations for his death. The reason was simple: the death of an ally deserved to be compensated, because he came to help fight off the enemy. It was argued that there were no grounds to pay reparations for the death of an enemy, after all, he had come to kill them. (Kopio Toe Lambu, Yakani Timali clan, Lenge, 1988)

This situation was to change as the population grew. Until approximately the mid-1800s, land in most parts of Enga was plentiful; clans could fight and disperse within tribal land or migrate to join groups in other areas where they prospered. As the land filled, it was no longer so easy for entire clans to move. Moreover, many groups received substantial support in times of peace from their "brother" clans as allies in warfare, in-laws and partners in exchange, support that was cut off in times of war. War deaths reduced the male labor force and was brutal on women and household economies:

> Even though our place was completely destroyed, I had to go back and make new gardens. I only worked there during the day and went back to my daughter's house at night. When I was working there, I sometimes felt lonely and looked around with tears running down my cheeks as I thought to myself, "Is this the way my place used to be or is it different now?" No people were moving around, the ring-barked trees were drying up and the grass was growing in the destroyed gardens. These things upset me so much that some-times when I had been working in my old gardens, I just didn't feel like eating. People are made to live in their environment, and when it is destroyed, we feel that we are nobody. (Apupuwana, Kaimaniwan clan, Kaiap, 1986)

As it became less advantageous to fight with the neighbors and disperse, ways were sought to reestablish peace and profitable social and economic exchange through the payment of compensation. The blueprint was in reparations to allies that were extended to an enemy in order to make peace after war (Wiessner and Tumu 1998). The following is a description from the Timali clan of central Enga of their first peacemaking ceremony following the cold-blooded murder of Loene, the son of a leader:

> Loene had seen the Sane men and went over to meet them. Unaware of the danger, he greeted them. He was given no time to think before the Sane men took up their spears and pierced Loene. After receiving several spear wounds, the poor man fell and then died. Soon after the incident, the Timali men found out about his death and made plans to start a tribal fight.
>
> After the fighting had stopped, confusion reigned, for the brother clans of Sane and Timali had never fought before. Wambi, the victim's brother, stepped forward and arranged what [is] said to have been Timali's first payment of compensation to enemy for men lost in battle. Attempts were then made to settle the conflict; both clans made reciprocal demands for compensation. It was a delicate process. Initiatory and mediatory words were spoken before the exchange of pigs and other valuables took place. Bushes were cleared and the ceremonial grounds were prepared for the compensation ceremonies to follow. Loene's murder set a precedent for peacemaking for the Timali clan. (Kopio Toea Lambu, Timali clan, 1988)

7.3 The Peace Process

For both war and peacemaking in intergroup conflicts, clan meetings were held to decide whether to go to war or solve the matter peacefully through compensation payments, or, in the case of war, to terminate hostilities through compensation (Sackschewski et al. 1970). All adult male clan members participated in weighing risks and benefits; each man was urged to express his opinion about going to war and possible impacts on his family. After much discussion, clan leaders orchestrated a consensus: to fight or settle through compensation (Young 2004). Women who married in from enemy clans were the first to privately explore openings for peace by visiting relatives in their natal clans and feeling out prevailing sentiments (Kyakas and Wiessner 1992). When peace seemed within reach, they informed their male relatives, who in turn made the initial overtures for peace. Reparations to both allies and enemy followed a set procedure:

1. *Saandi pingi*. Informal initiatory gifts given in private by bereaved allies or families in the clan of victim to request reparations. Acceptance of *saandi pingi* gifts committed a clan to paying compensation.

2. *Kepa singi*. The first payment of compensation was composed of steamed pork distributed in public on the clan's ceremonial ground by the owners of the fight to bereaved allies, or, in the case of enemy, to the clan of the victim. Much of the meat went to the family of the deceased.

3. *Saandi pingi or Yangenge*. Initiatory gifts of pigs/piglets, axes, salt and other goods and valuables given in private by the clan of the victim to the clan of the killer to oblige the payment of live pigs, *akali buingi*. The killer's clan tried to be very friendly and diplomatic, for they respected the victim's clan with a certain sense of fear of a payback murder. In such situations the value of pigs was not regarded highly – the life of a person was more important. (Lemonnier 1990) (Figure 10)

4. *Akali buingi*. Formal payment in public on the clan's ceremonial ground of live pigs, cassowary, axes, salt, or other goods and valuables by owners of the fight to families in the allied clan or enemy clan who had given initiatory gifts. For two years, members of the clan of the deceased would periodically give more initiatory gifts to families in the clan of the killer. The men from the killer's clan would then say that the slit-eared pigs they had raised for the compensation were growing old and it was time that they paid war reparations. They must have additional pigs to give away; that is, they not only had to settle the debt from the initiatory gifts, but give an extra pig on top of that. War reparations carried out in this manner were regarded as satisfying by the clan of the victim and others in the area . . . It is said that in some cases they were so happy that they went over and embraced the men from the killer's clan. The Enga had no word for peace, only "the breaking of the spear."

Figure 10 Tying pigs for war reparations (courtesy of Don Jeffers, mid-Lai 1960s)

The payment of war reparations was the collective responsibility of the whole clan, not just a matter for leaders. A person who had received a number of initiatory gifts was expected to give two or three additional pigs. One of the fundamental features of *akali buingi* was the additional or "profit" pigs given to individuals in the victim's clan. Although the compensation process stretched out over two or more years, peace was maintained by the expectation of financial gain while the healing hands of time went to work. All families tried to do well in contributing; those who did gained respect, though overt competition between clan members was discouraged. Families had the right to choose to whom in the clan of the victim their pigs would go. Those who were recalcitrant were cajoled into contributing. Multiple ties between individuals in the two warring clans were thus formed. The recipients of live pigs had their pig herds restocked, unlike in many highland PNG societies where only butchered pork was distributed. (Feil 1982).

The adoption of peacemaking through compensation to the enemy was gradual and dependent on the circumstances around each particular war. In Meggitt's (1977: 137) study of war reparations paid to the enemy for men killed in wars between circa 1900 and 1955, three out of twenty-eight (11 percent) enemy deaths in wars between "brother" clans were not compensated in contrast to sixteen out of thirty-six (44 percent) for deaths of enemies from other tribes. After more accurately dating the wars recorded by Meggitt, we found that percent of deaths from enemy tribes that were not compensated for during the 1900–50 period would have been significantly lower (Wiessner 2010b). The increased need for pigs and other forms of wealth was partially met by affinal and maternal kin who came forward to help. The necessity to compensate enemy deaths led to many rules to contain warfare and limit damage so as not to incur exceedingly high costs: do not harm or kill women and children, do not burn women's houses, do not rape women, do not mutilate corpses, do not kill in cold blood or finish off the wounded, and do not kill someone on another clan's land.

When restorative measures were extended to the enemy for peacemaking, a new arena was opened for big-men to gain influence because of the importance of many nonmaterial contributions in peacemaking such as oration, wealth management, mediation and bringing about consensus. These skills allowed big-men to give substantial benefits to many at a relatively low cost to themselves. They held meeting after meeting to assure that the reparations would be distributed to satisfy everybody in the clan of the victim (Wiessner 2019). Even after the last payments had been paid, big-men had to make up the difference to those who received little and were dissatisfied. The following account gives a sense of the complexities:

> The word of peace from the killer's clan was of utmost importance. However, if the clan of the victim was met in a different way, such behavior did not go unheeded. For instance, the killer's clan might say that they didn't want the victim's clan to come and ask for reparations and ridicule them by saying that they did not invite the victim to come and fight, that the poor man brought on his own fate and deserved to die. Such words were very provocative. Even if they were not said in front of the victim's clan but leaked out, the victim's clansmen would become furious.
>
> When a person was killed, he was gone forever. You would miss him always. His bed would be empty and his fellow clansmen, upon seeing the empty bed, would be overcome by emotion and feel like going out to avenge his death . . . To prevent such feelings, one had to go and remove his bed from sight, get rid of his pipe, dispose of his netbag, and anything that would remind people of him . . . Only when his clan was paid war reparations would they slowly forget the death of the person killed in the war . . .
>
> You see, not all people in the victim's clan would be satisfied with the war reparations, and a poor person in the clan was most likely to miss out . . . The big-man of a clan had to make sure that no dissatisfied person would think of taking revenge for he did not want to see chaos come to his place and did not want the houses and gardens to be destroyed. For such reasons the big-man had to give a pig, preferably one which he had decided to keep for himself, to the person who was most likely to cause trouble. (Kyakas Sapu, Lanekepa clan, Wabag, 1991)

War reparations ended hostilities by compensating loss of life and reestablishing balance of power. Unfortunately, peacemaking did not include agreements about land gained or lost, leaving open the possibility for ongoing contestation. Land gained was left empty for years because of continuing tensions; land lost was often regained in subsequent wars or returned after a payment.

7.4 The Exchange of Gifts and Blows

Throughout Enga history, armed conflicts were inseparable from economic exchange that compensated losses and restored balance of power. In the wars of the earlier generations, opponents were driven out to settle in another portion of tribal land or totally evicted by the victors and allies. Around the fifth generation, when land was no longer so abundant and it was often not desirable to displace neighbors, significant changes began to take place. Either armed hostilities had to continue indefinitely at a high cost to both parties or reparations had to be paid to allow clans to fight, make peace and stay put. Governance over war and peace were in the hands of community during clan meetings, but brought into practice by big-men who were influential in shaping outcomes and lauded for their successes. By "eating the food of war reparations," peace was reestablished, not merely as the absence of war but as active communication, economic exchange and intermarriage of benefit to most families. The payment of war reparations to enemy stimulated production in all clans of Enga, not just those with central roles in major ceremonial exchange systems.

Clans went to war with the full realization that wealth would be required for conflict resolution, that they would have to produce pigs for the purpose and ask relatives outside the clan to help raise payments. The close association of warfare and exchange for peacemaking allowed warfare to be manipulated to pursue assertive goals – reestablishing balance of power, taking land or eliminating competitors – but also affiliative ones such as creating exchange ties (Knauft 1990). Meanwhile, the larger economic systems that were in their early stages by the fifth generation – the Tee cycle, the Great Wars and the Kepele cult network – were all dependent on the establishment of internal and external peace and balance of power for wealth to flow. Restorative measures within and between clans thus established the conditions for the expansion of the political economy.

8 The Convergence of the Great Wars, Tee Cycle and Kepele Cult

> The Tee is like a great river which flows out of the past through the lives of Enga.
> (Maua Pakiala, Yambatane Watenge Clan, Saka valley)

By the fifth generation, payments of war reparations to enemies were stimulating the surplus economy throughout Enga, the Kepele cult was expanding in western areas, and the Great Ceremonial Wars (Great Wars) were being fought with ever-increasing popularity in central Enga. The Tee Cycle encompassed but a sparse network of clans along three trade routes radiating out from the Saka valley in the east. It was a system of finance from the onset that provided wealth to meet the needs of participants, whether these be bridewealth, control of the trade or war reparations. Three generations later, it was a flooding river of wealth swept through virtually every clan of eastern and central Enga. Could a family from the fifth generation have taken a journey through time to attend a Tee Cycle festival of their great-grandchildren in the mid-twentieth century, they would have been astonished at what they saw. Rather than the expected thirty to fifty pigs, hundreds would stand tethered to stakes on the ceremonial grounds; previously scarce pearlshells would be distributed in numbers inconceivable to them. Standing amid thousands of participants and spectators from clans far removed from the Tee in their time, they would marvel at the wealth and display of the Great Kamongo, big-men who were major managers of the Great Wars and Tee Cycle. How did this come to be?

Part of the answer lies in the exchange of ideas and wealth that had long tied eastern, central and western Enga together despite their very different post–sweet potato developments. The Great Wars were built on existing practices, namely fighting and paying war reparations to allies, which turned such competition into dramatic and ritualized tournaments. Due to the sheer number of participants, the Great Wars constructed vast exchange networks fueled by intensified home production within a broad segment of the population. The glamour, excitement and ceremony of these tournaments conferred greater social and symbolic value on pigs and mobilized households to step up production for the exchanges. Nonetheless, the Great Wars were fueled by home production and lacked the chains of finance of the Tee Cycle.

For quite some time the Tee Cycle and the Great Wars ran parallel to one another (Map 6); however there were Great Kamongo in central Enga whose clans participated in both (Wiessner and Tumu, 1998: chapter 11). Drawing on their fund of knowledge and reputation from performance in the Great Wars, the Great Kamongo effectively campaigned to lengthen Tee chains and the cycles of Tee to deliver wealth for Great War exchanges. When opportunities arose, the Great Kamongo, drew pigs from the Tee Cycle to help fund the Great Wars and channeled pigs coming out of the Great War exchanges to repay their Tee partners to the east. Once connected, both networks flourished. Historical narratives and genealogies indicate that families of emerging elites intermarried to secure their hold on the two exchange systems (Wiessner 2010b).

Coordinating the Tee Cycle and Great Wars both lengthened Tee chains and substantially increased the wealth circulating throughout eastern and central

Enga. At that time a new system for counting pigs emerged, one that differed from that used by the neighboring Melpa Moka, surpassing the old system that went up to twelve based on body parts. Its origin is unclear. It allowed people to count by twos up to forty to achieve one bundle of pigs and then start again with a second bundle of forty with the capacity to go up into the hundreds. The new counting system was used only for individual contributions, not for wealth distributions of entire clans, because unlike the Melpa Moka system, the Tee Cycle was not an institution for competitive reciprocal gifting between clans. Rather individuals and cooperated to move wealth through the cycle, striving to do well in Tee exchange to build reputation; big-men competed with others in their own clans and leaders in other clans to gain prestige as renowned managers of wealth.

8.1 Pearlshells Enter the Tee Cycle

Other developments resulted from competition in the expanding Tee Cycle. Great Kamongo in eastern Enga were challenged by the fact that everybody could compete as long as pigs were the major currency. They sought to consolidate their advantage by valuing pearlshells that could be obtained only through far-reaching social networks. Pearlshells were not unknown to Enga but were extremely rare until they began to be integrated into bridewealth and war reparation exchanges in the Kandep area of southern Enga around the fifth generation. By the fourth generation, pearlshells were included in the Tee Cycle and arrived in the adjacent populations of the Waghi valley (Hughes 1977: 193; Strathern 1971: 235–236).

Pearlshells were given new value by old means. They were integrated into bridewealth payments, war reparations and, importantly, into cults to promote fertility. One was the female spirit cult with its parade of pearlshells that was imported into eastern Enga from the south and directed at an asexual spirit woman who came to men as a bride to bring fertility to their families without the risk of female menstrual contamination (see Figure 11). The central theme of the cult was appropriate for the burgeoning Tee Cycle in which men and women were separated but indissolubly linked (Strathern 1970). The cult spread rapidly in eastern Enga, but at the western end of the network, pearlshells had much less appeal (Leahy and Crain 1937: 254; Meggitt 1974; Wirz 1952), in part because the big-men of central Enga sought a supply of pigs to help finance the Great Wars as well as high quality axes essential for production.

> Some of the pearlshells were regarded as so precious that people could even start a tribal war over them. Women fall in love at the very sight of a pearlshell of this kind. Several pigs could be given in exchange for one of them. Such

Figure 11 The parade of pearlshells in the female spirit cult (courtesy of Don Jeffers, mid-Lai valley, 1966)

pearlshells would go [from the upper Minamba valley] to the Saka valley but that is as far as they would go, the reason being that people further up the valley do not like pearlshells so much ... Therefore I would return the pearlshells eastward to Timbai and Kola and send westwards via the Saka things that were desired by people further to the west – for example, stone axes used for both ceremonial and practical purposes. (Kepa Pupu, Yoponda clan, Minamb valley, 1990)

The adoption of pearlshells by the Melpa Moka developed along a different trajectory. The Melpa obtained pearlshells via chains of big-men to the south, such that big-men with appropriate connections could maintain a monopoly on the procurement of pearlshells (Strathern 1971). This advantage changed the balance of power in the prestige economy, allowing big-men to consolidate power and facilitate its transmission (Feil 1982; Strathern 1971).

8.2 Coordination of the Tee Cycle and Great War Exchanges

For one or two generations, big-men of three focal tribes of central Enga succeeded in keeping the Tee Cycle and Great Wars apart so that their clans would be the only links between the two exchange systems. Such a monopoly put them in a position to strategically invest wealth from one system to the other:

We did not want these people to see our source of pigs. Those places [where the Great Wars were held] were our source of pigs referred to as our "Tee tree" in figurative speech. I am talking about places like the land of Malipini, Kamaniwane, Bia, Maioma and all the others directly to our north. We told them that these places were the lands of savages. We did so because we did not want them to see these places; if they did it would have weakened our position. (Kyakasa Sapu, Lanekepa clan, Lupamanda [Wabag], 1990; from discussion of why Yanaitini big-men told Tee Cycle organizers from clans to the east not to go north of Tetemanda)

Merging the Great Wars and Tee Cycle posed problems of coordination, cooperation and timing that threatened to foil the efforts of even the most astute organizers. The Great Wars had their own momentum from the spirit of opposition and their exchanges could not always be timed to fit the cycle of the Tee. The Tee, by contrast, required intensive campaigning on the part of Great Kamongo to reach an agreement across many clans to launch a cycle that would connect with the Great Wars. Given the number of clans involved, the communities dispersed over rugged landscape and the conflicting interests at different points in the cycle, this task was in this context that a version of the Kepele ancestral cult, imported from western Enga into some tribes of central Enga at an earlier date and practiced at a small scale, was transformed into quite a different institution and renamed Aeatee or Pokalya (Map 5).

8.3 The Aeatee Cult

For Yanaitini clans located at the western terminus of the Tee Cycle, the Aeatee and its elaborate feasting had six phases spread out over four or more years. These were organized during clan meetings and directed toward tribal unity by evoking the power of the ancestors to improve the future of all celebrants (Table 4). As in the Kepele, all men had to provide one pig each for the feasts to underwrite equality. Through the Aeatee, rifts within Yanaitini were mended and tensions assuaged between clansmen over growing social inequalities. Celebrants were reminded that their successes would be turned not only to promote their own names but also to provide for the needs of their fellow group members. Once unity was established, broader-scale economic plans could be realized.

The association between the Aeatee and the Tee Cycle in the Yanaitini tribe was constructed with such care that the general public saw fertility and prosperity as the sole goal of the cult. Distribution of food within the Aeatee was not directly related to other economic ventures: marsupials hunted and pork from pigs raised for the various stages by Yanaitini households were given out freely to celebrants and guests without incurring or discharging debts for a former Tee Cycle. The atmosphere of solidarity was not ruptured by displays of big-men or political speeches.

Table 4 Relationship between the Tee Cycle, Aeatee ceremonies and Great Wars.

Aeatee ritual	Tee Cycle	Great Wars
Phase 1		
Prepare materials for Aeatee house.		
Marsupial feast. Yanaitini united.		
Phase 2		
Prepare ceremonial grounds. Marsupial feast. Tee organizers come up from east.	*Saandi Pingi*: initiatory gifts of piglets, pork, goods and valuables sent east with Tee organizers.	Wealth from Great Wars used for initiatory gifts in Tee Cycle.
Phase 3		
House construction, pork feast, Tee organizers come from east	More initiatory gifts sent east.	Same as above.
Phase 4		
Fertility rites, marsupial feast, Yanaitini united.		
Phase 5		
Rites for ancestral stones, pork feast, Tee organizers set off for the east to request the main gifts in the Tee.	*Tee Pingi*: Main gifts sent from east to west.	Main gifts channeled into Great War exchanges.
Phase 6		
Burning of Aeatee house and pork feast. Yae Phase of Tee Cycle begins.	*Yae Pingi*: Butchered pork from west to east.	Great War opponents compete to burn Aetee house. Great War pork sent east in Yae Pingi.

Great Kamongo from eastern Enga came to celebrate and observe. During the Aetee, Yanaitini demonstrated to Tee cycle organizers from the east that they had the wealth and unity to launch a Tee Cycle. They later drew up plans in the seclusion of men's houses. The various stages of the Aeatee kept the cooperative spirit alive within Yanaitini throughout one entire Tee Cycle and fixed points in time for the different phases of the cycle to begin and end (Table 4). In short, economic and political strategies unfolded in the shadow of the Aeatee; though the Aeatee and cycles of the Tee were not directly intertwined, they were mutually dependent. Women did not participate in the rituals but obtained large amounts of pork from the feasts and joined in celebrations outside the ritual area.

The final phase of the Aeatee was dramatic. Preparations were made to burn the Aeatee house and the biggest feast of all was held, attracting spectators from Tambul, the Saka, the Lai and Lagaip valleys and the Kandep area . Once again the grass was ceremoniously trampled by night in preparation. The house was not burned by Yanaitini, but by the "owners of the war" in the Great War between the Malipini and the Itapuni who competed to set it aflame. Contenders woke just before dawn, approached the house stealthily, set fire to the house and slipped away. Men pursued the "culprits," shooting arrows and engaging in mock battle. The burning of the Aeatee cult house and subsequent feast attended by all marked the beginning of pig kills for the Yae phase of the Tee Cycle. From start to finish the Aeatee could take four years or longer to complete.

Similar fertility cults, the female spirit cult and the Polaoanda, were held at the eastern terminus of the Tee cycle with comparable goals. The following account describes the final phase of the Polaoanda held by the Yambetane tribe of the Saka valley in eastern Enga detailing who participated, how pork was given freely and later how big-men would gather to plan the Tee Cycle.

Man, this was a great event! Before the ceremonies began, word was sent to all the areas. The Yambatane tribe would announce that on the next day the slitting of the pigs' ears would take place to mark them for Tee exchange. After the news reached all the areas, people would come to the Saka valley from all directions for the cult feast. They would arrive in full dress and take part in the pork feast, bringing net bags with them to carry home the remaining pork, for many sides of pork were given to guests at the feast . . . Then all the people from the west would come down. During the feast when a person was given pork, he would share it with a friend – sometimes pork would be given to a person one had never met before. In this way pork circulated to all those who attended the feast. They carried home the pork that they had received directly from relatives.

Question: Was the Tee Cycle discussed at this time?
Yes, that is what we did. One person from each clan would be present in the men's house . . . When all were present, one person would ask on behalf of all of the guests why the Watenge clan had performed their cult. They would ask about their pigs. Were they fully grown? When were they going to hold *Tee Pingi* [the phase of main gifts]? When would they kill pigs for the *Yae* [the last phase of butchered pork]? They held long discussions on the subject of the Tee cycle and finally agreed on a time to start the *Tee Pingi* or *Yae*, whichever it might be. (Apanyo Maua, Watenge clan, Saka Laiagam, 1988)

The popularity of the Great Wars grew until the costs became formidable in terms of production, time expended and, to a lesser extent, lives lost. For Great War leaders, the Tee Cycle promised the possibility to manage ever more wealth at a lower cost. Moreover, the Tee could not be concealed forever as it expanded and became more prominent. Great War leaders began to see the Tee as a potential alternative to forge exchange ties and made efforts to join. Likewise, some big-men involved in the Tee realized it would be to their advantage to replace the Great War networks with Tee routes. One by one, the exchange routes built during the Great Wars were subsumed by the Tee Cycle (Map 6). Only when they were convinced that they could get the same things that they were getting in the Great Wars did they give them up to join the Tee Cycle. At the time of contact with Europeans, this great exchange network involved most clans of eastern and central Enga – more than 200 clans and 30,000–70,000 participants (Brennan 1982; Wiessner and Tumu 1998). The river of Tee had flooded, fed by its many tributaries.

9 Leadership

> They say there are men named Kuku and Aa
> Yopene and Kakapone from Yakangemai.
> What makes them who they are?
> What makes them as renowned as they are?

The vast systems of exchange, ritual and warfare could not have emerged without the agency of strong leaders. The verse from bachelors' cult poetry just quoted asks how great leaders came to be extremely influential in a political system despite the strong principle of potential equality, the question to be addressed in this section. To understand the rise of leadership, let us first consider the natural resources that enabled or constrained pathways to prestige, as it is the character of the storable surplus wealth that structures the strategies chosen and the nature of exchange (Sahlins 1972: 215). What forms of wealth were available to aspiring households?

Pigs, the major source of wealth, required substantial care and supplementary feeding; up to two-thirds of the sweet potato crop was fed to pigs at the height of the Tee Cycle, but a single household could not raise more than five to ten pigs at one time (Waddell 1972: 66). Pearlshells as prestige items could be used to consolidate power; however, they were of little utilitarian value and not highly prized throughout Enga (Leahy and Crain 1937: 254; Wirz 1952). Other valued items such as axe stone and salt circulated widely in the trade but were not abundant enough to be used as currencies to heavily indebt others. It was labor, not land, that was short, so it was often more advantageous to build ties of cooperation with neighbors to obtain wealth through exchange than to take land through warfare, defend it and cultivate it (Sillitoe 1977). No evidence exists that families of *kamongo* had more land than others in their clans (Meggitt 1974: 191n43), nor could they appropriate the labor of fellow clanspeople without reciprocation. The salt springs, a major source of wealth, were located in high-altitude areas where the owners could not live year-round to defend the pools; there was more to gain from exchange with those who came to make salt.

Given these limitations, the path to stronger leadership depended to a large extent on intangible assets: ability to bring about consensus in clan meetings, regional knowledge, social ties, skills in oratory and the effective management of wealth, as well as a reputation for generosity and reliability.

9.1 A Family History of Leadership

We are fortunate to be able to follow developments in leadership via a five-generational family history from the Yakane Timali clan of central Enga describing the gradual developments in leadership that arose hand in hand with the growing economy (Wiessner and Tumu 1998). The more detailed episodes begin around 1850 with the life of Wambi. The following account describes one of his early wealth distributions, emphasizing how leaders of his time maintained a modest stance.

> Although Wambi was the first leader of our clan [ca. 1850], according to what my grandfather said, his leadership was fairly weak. He did not have strong influence, but merely made comments and suggestions. There was no pig exchange on a large scale in the time of Ipawape, Yambukana and his son Wambi. There were pork feasts, but only with neighboring clans. During the lifetime of Wambi, the pig exchange called *tee* only involved the exchange of goods between neighboring [allied] clans for war reparations ... The great pig exchange, the Tee Cycle that we know today, began in the lifetime of Kepa, the son of Wambi. Wambi's first public distribution of wealth was during a war reparation exchange [to the enemy]. All other members of the Timali clan also gave away pigs, but Wambi gave away more than the others. His row of pig stakes was longer than all the rest. There was nothing exciting or dramatic about our first *tee* exchange – for example, Wambi and his men did not sing any boasting songs, he did not wear any intricately woven bird of paradise feathers on his wig, nor did he make eloquent speeches. (Kopio Toea Lambu, Timali clan, Lenge, 1987)

Kopio's accounts of Wambi's sons move into a fascinating time when the Tee Cycle was expanding, allowing people to assemble far more wealth at one place at one point in time than by home production alone.

> In Kepa's lifetime Tee Cycles were held, but they were short ones. What is told of Kepa's participation in the Tee begins when the phase of the main gifts [*tee pingi*] was already complete and the *mena yae* phase involving large pig kills and the distribution of pork was about to follow ... Kepa owned a lot of

large pigs, some of which were too fat to enter the doorway of his house. He left them roaming around the courtyard of his house and fed them there.

The great *yae* phase of the Tee began and soon it was Timali's turn to slaughter pigs at Lenge. Many pigs were killed on this occasion, and as expected, many potential recipients turned up that day. All the necessary preparations had been made, but the number of pigs to be steamed in the rectangular earth oven was so great that they ran out of leaves, stones and firewood . . . Most of the people who came that day were from the west, some of whom were Kepa's exchange partners or associates. There was so much pork to eat! Kepa himself killed about twenty pigs . . . and some of the meat rotted before it was consumed and had to be thrown into the Lai river . . .

During the Tee Cycle that followed that *yae*, Kepa planted his stakes on the ceremonial grounds in a single line. His row of pigs was the longest. In this phase of the Tee, Kepa counted his pigs. The counting system went like this: two, four, six, eight, ten, twelve, and so on. Kepa was the first Timali *kamongo* to apply the new counting system. After all the pigs were counted, casuarina trees were planted at each end of the line to mark its length.

It is said that my grandfather Kepa did not wear a headdress of bird of paradise feathers nor did he boast. Kepa did not sing any songs about how wealthy he was. He wanted to be friends with everybody and was very cautious not to create bad feelings among his people, especially with his Tee partners. It is said that in this Tee Cycle, Kepa gave away about sixty pigs. It was in the time of Kepa that stronger leaders began to emerge towards the end of his lifetime . . . All of these things happened following one important event: the introduction of the counting system. Before, nobody really knew for sure who was the real *kamongo* [big-man]. When the counting system was introduced [origin unknown], people were able to tell who was the real *kamongo*. The Tee and strong leadership grew together and reinforced each other. This did not happen overnight. (Kopio Toea Lambu, Timali clan, Lenge, 1987)

Kepa's son Pendaine was renowned for channeling wealth to and from the Tee Cycle to the Great Wars and eventually helped engineer the replacement of Great Wars and their exchange routes by extending Tee Cycle routes. Everybody we interviewed along Tee routes had heard his name. Unlike his forefathers and more contemporary big-men, he married only one wife. His wife told him that unless he was too sexually passionate, there was no need to marry a second woman – his pigs would not go hungry and she could do all the necessary work. And she did. His family increased home production by giving out pigs to people in neighboring clans for care in exchange for some of the piglets born. He welcomed war refugees, people with disabilities and unmarried young women who sought education in the household of a renowned *kamongo* and made contributions to their bridewealth. He was a quiet man of few words; however, when he spoke everybody listened attentively. The following is an excerpt from Kopio's description of the organization of the Tee Cycle in Pendaine's time:

A week before the Tee was to take place at Lenge, Pendaine held meetings on the [Timali] ceremonial ground. He explained to the crowd how he had carried out the campaign for the Tee Cycle and told his Tee associates from the east what he would like them to do with the Tee when it reached their clans. Endless debates were held from morning to evening. His Tee associates more or less approved of his plans, but his jealous rivals sat in the midst of the crowd carefully listening to catch any flaws in his speeches ... Pendaine spoke low and little, yet the crowd held their breath when he opened his mouth to speak. He was an awesome figure with a towering build that naturally attracted attention ... The meetings went on for a week. During this time the people from distant places were accommodated at Lenge. Pendaine's Tee partners stayed in his men's house and those who lived nearby went home for the night.

The long account then describes a Tee ceremony in Timali, Pendaine's clan. A few things are noteworthy: (1) the emphasis on Pendaine's appearance; (2) all clan members were similarly dressed and engaged in counting and giving away their own pigs; (3) Pendaine's emphasis on his own home production as well as success in managing the Tee Cycle; (4) Pendaine was grooming his only son, Lambu, to follow him; (5) recipients often gave away pigs immediately after receiving them to meet their own financial obligations and to limit the size of their pig herds; (6) the distribution of other forms of wealth was held after the all-important pig distribution; and (7) a new counting system was used.

The great Pendaine was dressed to perfection from head to toe. It was midday and his body glistened under the sun's rays. Because of his tall stature, his plumes seemed to touch the sky ... On one hand, his appearance was awesome, powerful, and glorious; on the other, he made a savage and fierce impression.

The great Yakani *kamongo* Pendaine appeared on the scene. As he walked through the rows of stakes towards the center of the ground he said in a loud voice, "Auu!" All eyes were fixed upon him and, as the expression goes, even the frogs down by the Lai river stopped croaking. There was complete silence. It was broken by a sudden commotion in the back of the crowd at the eastern end and the sound of marching feet [as the pigs were brought on to the ceremonial ground]. Pendaine moved over to the first stake after he saw that everything was going well.

"I have campaigned for this Tee Cycle," he said. "People of the east, please listen to what I have to say. I have gone to the Sau and to the upper Lai to get this Tee Cycle. I have followed my word. I have done this so that you can hold the *Yae* [return phase] for me and the people of the west ... "

After the speech Pendaine signaled to one of his fellow clansmen to count his pigs. Pendaine, the counter and several others made their way down to the end of his row of stakes. Young Lambu followed at their heels. When they reached the end, they started counting the pigs. Every Timali participant in the *Tee* did the same: each made a short speech and each counted his own pigs. Pendaine's team kept counting on since his row was the longest.

> After this was done the recipients untied the pigs and led them off the ceremonial grounds. Those from neighboring clans who received many pigs then planted their stakes in the ground, tied the pigs to them, and gave them away on the spot ... After some time, the pigs were out of sight, and Timali clansmen gathered on the ceremonial grounds once again. This time they gave away cassowaries, stone axes, and minor items of wealth like beads, and shell-embroidered headbands ... The great Tee festival was finally over at Lenge. (Kopio Toea Lambu, Timali clan, Lenge, 1987)

Lambu, Pendaine's son, grew up in quite a different political and economic setting. Born around 1900, Lambu never experienced the Great Wars of his own tribe, only those of tribes to the west. He first participated in the Tee Cycle when it drew large amounts of wealth from the Great War exchanges. When the Great War between the Malipini-Potealini and the Itapuni-Awaini was supplanted by the Tee Cycle in the late 1930s or early 1940s, many new feeder routes were added, greatly complicating the timing and course of the Tee Cycle. Tee Cycle chains composed of cooperating big-men from different clans had different strategies for the timing and course of the cycle, creating a new and sometimes ruthless level of competition.

Lambu was a very different character than his father, Pendaine: competitive, politically aggressive and flamboyant. When Lambu reached maturity, his father arranged for him to marry three wives at once, an unprecedented event. In years to come he married another nine women in the process of building his "Tee empire." Here is an account from his son:

> Before I go further, recall that my father had many wives, well, he also had many servants [or workers]. They did a wide range of jobs for him including looking after his pigs, fencing, making gardens, and building houses ... [he goes on to list many other activities]. During the Tee cycle one of his servants would leap down his row of pigs to express his elation and success, because Lambu was too heavy to run and leap for that distance ... In return for their labor, Lambu looked after his servants. Most of them came from neighboring clans but some were married and came from far away. He allotted them plots of land so that they could support their families and gave them pigs. When their children married, he provided bridewealth. Most servants stayed for their entire lifetimes; others went back to their own clans after some time. Lambu gave them what they wanted, and they were generally satisfied and liked the Great Kamongo. If I am not mistaken, he had about thirty servants. (Kambao Toea Lambu, Timali clan, 1988)

To have a handful of helpers in the households of big-men was not new; however, the size of Lambu's household was unprecedented until the colonial period. Given the equality of clanspeople, helpers were almost always men from other clans – for example, war refugees, the poor or the disabled. Later in

Lambu's lifetime, the colonial administration and missions were to change the playing field, as will be discussed later.

9.2 Female Leaders

Throughout Enga historical traditions, men were influential in the public realm and women in the private realm. However, the influence of women increased as exchange systems grew, because women provided crucial ties between clans and did much of the work to produce pigs for exchange. Husbands and wives discussed to whom their pigs should be given and thereafter women brought the pigs they had raised to the ceremonial grounds and tied them to stakes. In some historical narratives, the names of the women who raised the largest pigs were called out during *tee* ceremonies. Only a few women became leaders in the Tee Cycle. One of these was the renowned Takime:

> Women were essential to men's success. Behind every successful man was a woman who raised pigs and cultivated social ties. In a very few cases exceptional women became leaders in their own right. The most notable was Takime, the daughter of the Yae Tee organizer, Yapao, of the Sikini Mangalya clan. Takime was born around 1911. Her husband, Lapinyo, from the Wapai clan, was killed in warfare when her two sons, Kekeo and Tumu, were less than five years old. She decided to take on the role of both wife and husband.
>
> Takime built fences, chopped firewood, planted sugarcane, fought in wars and helped negotiate peace. When Takime did women's work she wore women's clothing; when she did men's work she put on a man's apron, wrapped it between her legs and tied it to her belt in the back. The only event that she did not participate in was rituals for the ancestors. To increase her household standing she paid bridewealth for eleven "wives" for herself. These women later married men in her clan and assisted in her household. She lived in a men's house and built two longhouses where her "wives" and their husbands lived.
>
> Takime travelled widely with other *kamongo* to organize the Tee Cycle, sleeping in women's houses and convincing wives of Tee leaders to make her plans work. When Tee negotiations between men were taking too long, she would tell them to hurry up because she had to care for her children. When she returned home, she put on women's clothes and took on the role of mother. When the Tee Cycle reached her clan, she put on men's clothes and gave public speeches. Takime's guiding principle for success was to treat everybody, from a nobody to a Great Kamongo, with care and respect for what he or she had to give. She is alleged to have said: "Every person has something of value and must be treated with respect. Even a person who brings fleas into the house may be of value one day because the fleabites might wake you when your life is in danger." (Kekeo Yapao, Takime's son, Wapai Clan, Lakopena, 1989)

Takime's kindness, respect for others and contribution to the welfare of her clan is said to have won her praise from men. Such acceptance of uniqueness characterizes Enga culture and was a force behind change: innovation was welcomed if it brought benefits to the clan, particularly economic benefits. Her sons went on to become leaders in the Tee Cycle.

9.3 Hierarchy and Equality in Leadership

Relationships of equality and inequality in the full-blown precontact Tee Cycle were complex. At the top were the Great Kamongo, Great War and Tee Cycle managers, whose positions had been passed on in their families for one or more generations. Of eighty-four sons of Great Kamongo who survived to adulthood, thirty-two (38 percent) became Great Kamongo, eleven (13 percent) became lesser *kamongo* or wealthy men, forty-one (49 percent) became ordinary men (Wiessner 2010a). Thirty-eight of the eighty-four sons of Great Kamongo (45 percent) married the daughters of *kamongo* from other clans (Wiessner 2010a). Fathers did not choose specific sons to succeed them but observed their sons as they grew up; as they developed certain attributes, people would conclude that a certain son would succeed his father and encouraged him to do so. Nobody could name a Great Kamongo who lived before the colonial period who came from an ordinary or poor family, though some may have come from the families of lesser *kamongo*.

Five reasons were given for inheritance of leadership by capable sons (Wiessner 2010a): (1) sons of Great Kamongo acquired knowledge of networks by accompanying their fathers; (2) capable sons of Great Kamongo inherited Tee partnerships and were married to the daughters of other important leaders, keeping knowledge and influence within a limited circle of elites; (3) travel could be dangerous, so only those who had long-established networks for protection could travel widely; (4) the public looked to sons of Great Kamongo to follow their fathers, seeking continuity of leadership; widespread public support was essential for success (Wiessner and Tumu 1998: appendix 12); and (5) although Great Kamongo had no privileged access to the spirit world, they were major players in importing cults from neighboring groups to bring about change.

Beneath the Great Kamongo, who managed the large exchange networks, were lesser local *kamongo*, leaders of subclans, who were astute, hard-working and skilled in pig husbandry, wealthy and polygamous. Such men organized local events within the clan and between adjacent clans. Ordinary men who were productive could and did become lesser *kamongo* and competed with others in their clans or subclans for wealth and local influence. Lesser *kamongo* deferred to the Great Kamongo in the interest of group unity for important decisions pertaining to the major exchange cycles. Nonetheless, competition for status of lesser *kamongo* made for a highly competitive, productive and dynamic economy and kept community governance alive.

10 Outcome

> On one fine sunny day the taukopa beech trees will catch fire.
> Don't you see us drying up for the bush fire day?
> *(Song from Ain's cult)*

By the time Europeans entered Enga, the Kepele cult had spread throughout the west, the Great Wars in central Enga were drawing ever more participants from far and wide, and the Tee Cycle out of eastern Enga was expanding rapidly. As if that were not enough, throughout Enga the Sangai/Sandalu bachelors' cults, war reparation payments and celebrations for the spirit world required ever more resources. This section will explore the following questions: What were the reasons behind such growth? How was some degree of stability maintained? What were the outcomes?

First, the environment permitted almost unlimited agricultural growth. Most crops flourished in the fertile, well-watered soils, including sweet potatoes that permitted surplus production of pigs. The population was growing at approximately 1 percent per annum, adding more players with each generation and surplus was largely applied to building new forms of social integration (Wiessner and Tumu 1998). Second, ideals to compete, excel and gain status had prevailed in Enga society since the very earliest historical traditions and became accentuated through time with the growing economy. Third, the addition of pigs as a new currency for exchange, one that everybody could produce, altered the subsistence, exchange and prestige economies once the worth of pigs had been socially constructed (Modjeska 1982). Pigs then became essential for almost every event over the course of a lifetime.

A final force behind growth was the principle of equality within the genders. All men had rights to land and to support from clan members for a wide variety of needs, as well as control over the family's economic transactions together with their spouses. All women had rights to garden land through their husbands, support for building new gardens and a say over the distribution of pigs they had raised. Potential equality within the genders made it difficult for any individual to consolidate a broad hold on the means of production. Effective regulation of social, political and economic relations remained in the hands of community (Ostrom 1990). Outside of interclan decisions to organize the large exchange networks, decisions were made during clan meetings where every man had a say in efforts to maintain stability and trust in the face of a rapidly growing economy. Aspirations of those at the top and bottom of Enga society had to be aligned such that innovations in the exchange and prestige economies provided benefits for leaders and ordinary clan members, as well as exchange associates in other clans. Of course, leaders who knew how to play the system reaped more (Arnold 2004, 2009; Feinman 1995; Hayden 2011; Stanish 2010; Vaughn et al. 2010).

All societies have limits to unbridled competition and growth that at some point must lead to correction (Faulseit 2016) or collapse (Diamond 2005; Tainter 1988). This can occur for numerous reasons – for example, depletion of a resource base, unsustainable political complexity (Leach 1954), threats from neighboring groups or new resources and contacts that alter the balance of power. While collapse is well documented in more complex societies, what was the outcome in Enga?

10.1 The Great Wars

The Great Wars as the focus of interest and exchange for central Enga sowed the seeds of their own demise. Their popularity grew to the point where the majority of able-bodied men in a tribe or pair of tribes fought for months together with hosts and hundreds of allies. The costs were high in terms of time expended, wealth exchanged and, to a lesser extent, lives lost. The Yakani and Sene-Yokasa Great War was the first to end. Owners of the fight from both sides were already in the mainstream of the Tee Cycle, Yakani on the east–west route and Sene-Yokasa on the northern one (Map 6:4). Only the hosts, Aiyele and Pumane clans in the upper Sau valley, stood in the middle. Having seen how much wealth flowed in the Tee Cycle, they realized it could bring benefits similar to those of the Great Wars without the costs. After all, the original reasons for ritualizing fighting – to reestablish balance of power and exchange networks – had already been met. Consequently, around the turn of the nineteenth century, this Great War was discontinued and its exchange networks became fully integrated into the Tee cycle.

The other Great Wars did not give way to the Tee Cycle easily, but gradually came to an end between circa 1915 and 1945 because the the Wars provided unparalleled social excitement and opportunities for men, women and youths alike. They broke up the drudgery of everyday life, brought together people separated by steep mountains and valleys and were effective in moving wealth between different areas. Many of the participants removed from Tee Cycle routes had to be convinced that the Tee would provide benefits equal to those of the Great Wars. Approximately a decade after the Tee Cycle had supplanted the

Great War between the Yakani and the Sene-Yokasa, the last Great War was fought between the Lyaini-Sakalini and the Pumane-Aiyele, presumably because costs were high and similar benefits could be gained by joining neighboring Great Wars as allies (Map 6:1).

The conditions for the termination of the Great Wars between the Yanaitini and the Monaini Great Wars are clearer (Map 6:3). The Great War with the Monaini was particularly taxing since Yanaitini clanmen fought far from home. After an episode fought around 1915–20, Yanaitini paid their hosts in Sambe with some of the land in the Yandap that contained the renowned salt pools to end the war. The exchange networks between the Yanaitini and the Sambe, well developed by this time, allowed the Yanaitini to receive salt and other wealth from Sambe clans in exchanges and integrate it into the Tee Cycle.

The "die-hard" of the Great Wars was that between the Malipini-Potealini and the Itapuni-Awaini (Map 6:2). As the other Great Wars were phased out, this war drew greater attention and more participants. Since it was fought near the terminus of the Tee Cycle, wealth coming from the east could be used to finance the hosts on both sides and that flowing out of Great War exchanges could easily be reinvested. With few limits to growth, it escalated to the point where organization was exceedingly complex. In the last two episodes of this Great War, the battlegrounds and hosts were moved twice; after that clans who had hosted the Great Wars became full-fledged participants in the Tee Cycle and the owners of the fight followed suit. New routes were formed through clans along the ridge separating the Lai and Ambum and on into the northeast (Map 6 and Map 7).

> Those who took part in the Great Wars saw the large number of pigs that came in Tee Cycles held by people from the east. They thought that it was a good idea to join the Tee, so they stopped fighting and took part in the Tee. The trend to stop fighting and join the Tee was a fairly recent one; it took place in our time. However, down there along the Winikos route it had been in existence for some time. Tee Cycles had gone through this route but we, the people of the Ambum valley, did not know this. You see, during the Great Wars, people saw the large number of pigs coming through the Tee Cycle, stopped fighting, and began to participate in the Tee ... In this way the two Tee routes joined [i.e., the western and northern routes from the Saka valley]. (Auaka Taliu Waliu, Wailuni clan, Meriamanda/Ambum)

10.2 Reactions in Western Enga

Within the fertile environment of eastern and central Enga, the expansion of exchange networks was hampered only by conflicts of interest and organizational problems. The situation in the west, where soils were poorer, valleys steeper and altitudes higher, was quite different. Here, the population had experienced considerable disruption after the introduction of the sweet potato and increased surplus production to achieve social integration through exchange and ritual. They also became suppliers for the large ceremonial exchange systems to the east and were envious of the wealth that flowed in them. By the twentieth century the stress that had been mounting during the previous generations was evident in persistent warfare and the prevalence of leprosy and other illnesses. Some elders voiced dismay about the demand to produce large numbers of pigs for ritual, social and political occasions that in turn incited conflict over pigs and fertile garden land.

People in western Enga were also strongly influenced by the Dindi Gamu cult practiced from the Papuan Plateau through Huli areas to northern Enga, where natural gas leaks could be set alight during ceremonies (Frankel 1986). The Dindi Gamu, an ancient, secretive cult atypical of most Enga beliefs, required elaborate ritual and the feeding of a mythical fiery snake to stave off the apocalypse. When epidemics of human dysentery, pig pneumonia and severe frost and famine struck in the early 1940s, people felt that the apocalypse was drawing near (Gibbs 1977; Meggitt 1973; Wiessner and Tumu 2001). Moreover, tales of the arrival of Europeans, who were believed to be returning ghosts or "sky beings," circulated.

In the early 1940s, the ghost of a man named Aina appeared to his four sons at Yeim in northwestern Enga and instructed them how to avert the fiery apocalypse (Map 5). Aina and his sons launched a new cult movement, the Mata Katenge, in which the old ways were to be given up: menstrual practices, warfare, war reparations, bachelors' and ancestral cults and the Kaima and Kepele ceremonies for the ancestors (Wiessner and Tumu 2001). People were to shift away from fear of the ancestors and concentrate on the life energy given by the sun. Wambalipi and other prophets in the movement constructed high platforms to sacrifice pigs to the sun. If cult prescriptions were followed, giant pigs would appear, pearlshells would be found in pools, new crops would sprout in gardens and wealth would come to all. A cow's tail from the coast was circulated as evidence for the giant pigs. The Mata Katenge or Ain's cult spread rapidly, resulting in the slaughter of two-thirds of the pig population in western Enga and northeast through Kompiam. The fascinating permutations and transformations of Ain's cult as it spread are well described (Feil 1984; Gibbs 1977; Meggitt 1973; Wiessner and Tumu 2001). The cult was ended by Australian patrols and influential big-men when it reached Wabag. Big-men did not like the idea of riches for all to create a society of big-men (Meggitt 1973: 113). When the cult did not deliver, people found that they could not live in a world without exchange and resorted to exchanging feathers, forest goods, salt and other products until the pig population recovered (Feil 1983). It is hard to know which of the old ways would have been widely resumed, because soon after the cult collapsed missions arrived to bring many changes.

10.3 The Tee Cycle

During the lifetime of Kepa (Section 9) in the fifth generation, the Tee Cycle had only three routes converging at Saka Laiagam in eastern Enga and then moving to the western terminus at Tetemanda in central Enga following established trade routes (Map 7). The termination of the Great Wars and the addition of new exchange routes greatly altered the map of the Tee. Some 69 clans were added, creating routes running north and northeast from the western terminus at Tetemanda into areas rich in pigs – routes structured by pathways from the Great Wars. Tee Cycles required continual planning to coordinate 200–300 clans and synchronize the different routes for all three phases. Scores of big-men with their own grand plans became involved. Tee organizers in different clans then developed chains of allied partners who cooperated to channel cycles to their own advantage and competed with other such alliances. Competition thus occurred both between big-men of the same clan on different alliances and between chains of cooperators across clans to structure Tee Cycles to their advantage. The latter was a new development.

By the lifetime of Pendaine's son Lambu in the early 1950s, there were so many participants and divergent interests that obstructive strategies became standard practice: deceit, murder and instigation of tribal fights to block the cycles of Tee (see Nairn 1991 for the Moka). Even the most powerful big-men encountered great difficulties in executing their plans; they managed more wealth than the previous generation, but their positions were more tenuous. The following account from the late 1930s or early 1940s describes Lambu's efforts to launch a new cycle:

> The controversial Tee Cycle was about to take place and the *kamongo* from the east and west who were in favor of it allied with Lambu. Those who wanted it to take place at another time campaigned against them: Peke of the Sikini tribe and Yalona of the Yanaitini Piao clan were two of Lambu's rivals who vehemently opposed this Tee Cycle. The great debate for and against it began and a large meeting was held at Tilyaposa. In this meeting Lambu succeeded in convincing people to launch the Tee following his designs.
>
> ... My father began his speech saying, "People of the Mai [central Enga] want to do the Tee, but there are certain elements who are trying to discourage people from taking part. They are in effect dismantling our united stand in this matter. I would like to say this before the crowd: this person is like a witch who dances to and fro on a *sakae* rope. Be it known to you that the Mai are going to hold the Tee Cycle as you are already witnessing here today. Spread the word that the Mai will hold the Tee and the Yae to follow. Tell everyone that Lambu has said this." Then he took the *kapano* branch and *kola* grass

from me with such force that it almost knocked me over [Kambao, his son, circa twelve years old]. He took a step towards his greatest rival and threw the leaves at him saying, "Close your eyes forever. You will walk around no more." The great Sikini *kamongo* sat there humiliated in front of the entire crowd. (Kambao Lambu, Timali clan, Lenge, 1990)

Kambao goes on to tell how Sikini Peke, boiling with hatred, slipped into Pokalya, the sacred home of the Yakani ancestors, and cut a stem of *kyoo* bamboo to anger the ancestors and bring disaster to Lambu and his supporters. It is said that blood dripped from the severed stem. Upon its discovery, Lambu and his men pursued Peke but turned back when he crossed their clan boundary. Some months later, Peke was "mistakenly" shot by a man while tending his pigs in a zone of land vacated after warfare, an act attributed to Lambu's prophetic words, "Close your eyes forever. You will walk around no more!"

Though Lambu's accomplishments were greater than those who went before, their foundation was not as solid. The arrival of Europeans further complicated the situation. The missions put an end to the cults for the ancestors, the integrating institutions for organization of the Tee Cycle.[2] In the 1960s a ban on warfare, the Pax Australiana, reduced the need for wealth to pay war reparations. New forms of wealth coming from Europeans, steel, cash and hundreds of pearlshells made it possible for more individuals to reach the status of *kamongo*. Their positions were then formalized with appointments as *luluais* and *tultuls*, officers paid by the colonial administration, further freeing big-men from pressures to measure up to the qualities of traditional leaders (Meggitt 1974: 84).

Nonetheless, for two decades after contact the Tee Cycle flourished and expanded rapidly in all directions (Map 7) (Figure 12) until complications arose from the enormity of the network, accompanying organizational difficulties and, in some areas, increasing individualism (Feil 1984). The Tee no longer conformed to the standard cycle but was fragmenting. Boycotting of a cycle launched by one chain of collaborators became the rule rather than an exception. Lambu eventually gave up the Tee altogether and became a Seventh Day Adventist. After numerous false starts, the last Tee Cycle that swept through most of the network was launched in 1978–9. Initiatives to launch another cycle did not catch on. The reasons were many: other interests occupied the young and the Tee Cycle was no longer the major path to leadership and prosperity; success in government or business offered more opportunities in the monetary economy.

---

[2] I. E. Kleinig (1955). The significance of the Te in Enga culture. New Guinea Lutheran Mission Papers. Unpublished.

Figure 12 Yoponda Kepa wearing a feather headdress counting his line of pigs
(courtesy of Rev. Otto Hintze, Walya, early 1950s)

10.4 Closing Questions

Returning to the original question: what happens when people in a small-scale society with strong principles of equality are first able to produce a storable surplus? Multiple routes exist to institutionalized inequalities guided by history, existing institutions, environmental conditions, available resources and demography. The process was often gradual involving cycling between egalitarianism and hierarchy, as well as economic boom and bust (Earle 1997, 2011; Flannery and Marcus 2012; Kirsch and Rallu 2007; Kristensen 1987; Leach 1954; Price and Feinman 1995). Sweet potatoes arrived in Highland New Guinea to many linguistic groups sharing an emphasis on equality, big-man leadership, status competition, feasting, warfare, cults for the spirit world, ceremonies for young men, separation of men and women and far-reaching trade networks (Brown 1970, 1978; Feil 1987: table 5; Glasse 1969; Hayden 2014; Koch 1974; Lemonnier 1990; Modjeska 1982; Ploeg 1969; Rappaport 1968; Reay 1959; Ryan 1972; Sillitoe 1979; Strathern 1971). Why, then, did Enga systems of ceremonial exchange become so much larger and complex than those of other western highland societies in PNG with exception of the Melpa (Ketan 2004; Strathern 1971, 1979; Vicedom and Tischner 1943–8)?

A most significant factor was the diverse geographies, ecologies and cultural institutions within one linguistic group, which elicited different responses to the new crop by region, as well as the development of different institutions to apply surplus to ensuing social, economic and political challenges. The Kepele cult, Great Wars and Tee Cycle emerged more or less independently in response to local conditions, though all were fueled by surplus production. Although the large regional ceremonial exchange systems remained separate for some generations, the paths to link them were in place from the trade. The location of major salt springs in central Enga, a scarce resource in much of the PNG highlands, created vast unifying trade routes in all directions long before the arrival of the sweet potato. Moreover, the trade spurred initiatives such as Sangai/Sandalu bachelors' cults to standardize the norms and values that facilitated the marriages on which networks were built. The development and spread of ceremonies to pay compensation to the enemy, not present in many PNG highland societies, reduced the deaths, destruction of property and social ties that so inhibited economic growth. These conditions opened opportunities for enterprising men to cross boundaries and draw on the institutions of neighbors: the Great Wars for the production of large amounts of wealth, the Tee Cycle as a means of finance and redistribution of wealth, and the Kepele cult for the social technology to unite tribes, display strength and mitigate emerging inequalities.

A second factor was the innovative chains of finance that allowed individuals to concatenate partnerships in order to tap into wealth beyond the bounds of ordinary kinship reckoning, partially decoupling kinship from economic cooperation. Big-men in most highland PNG societies, whose wealth was based largely on household production, could assemble only 15–25 pigs for feasting, compensation and wealth distributions of raw or cooked pork (Brown 1978; Brown et al. 1990; Lederman 1986; Rappaport 1968; Salisbury 1962; Strathern 1969). By contrast, during more recent generations, some Great Kamongo distributed between 100 and 250 live pigs in the Tee (Bus 1951; Elkin 1953; Meggitt 1974). The distribution of live pigs rather than raw or cooked pork provided new pig stock for the recipients. Only the Melpa Moka also utilized chains of finance. However, since the Tee Cycle developed out of tactics to control the trade, it expanded over a much larger geographical area, while the Moka, which grew out of reciprocal war reparations, had limited geographical coverage (Strathern 1971, 1979). In the Moka, exchange partners competed, as in a potlatch, while in the Enga Tee, they cooperated to circulate wealth. Moreover, the major currency of the Moka was pearlshells procured by big-men with far-reaching networks, while the Tee Cycle remained largely furnished by pigs, allowing all families to participate.

A third factor behind the extraordinary growth of Enga ceremonial exchange was the strong social pressures exerted in the big-man system of leadership shaped by agency from both the bottom up and the top down. The position of big-man was attained and maintained through providing benefits to attract supporters, with every subclan and clan having competing leaders. Most decisions were thoroughly discussed in class meetings, fostering the trust necessary for exchange systems to expand and providing constant adjustment to meet the needs of different segments of the community. Strong social selection pressures for organizational skills and cooperation were also operative at the top between families of the Great Kamongo in different clans who organized the Great Wars, Tee Cycle and Kepele cult. The position of Great Kamongo were supported by intermarriage with others at the top; however, given pressures from the community, such intermarriage did not form closed circles of power.

> Another word of wisdom. A son of a Great Kamongo should marry the daughter of a poor man and vice versa [as a second or third wife]. The poverty of one becomes a liability to the other, and the prosperity of one becomes a blessing to the other. This is the way wealth was distributed and spread to many families. (Waima Waisa, Kalia clan, Wakumale village, 1988)

Such circulation of wealth stimulated most Enga to intensify production. Exchange systems grew so rapidly that adjustments were constantly called on by communities together with big-men to channel or regulate political and economic growth to maintain stability. By the 1930s, the economy was booming, leadership becoming partially inheritable, land was still plentiful and the environment was generous (Meggitt 1977: 183). One can only wonder: if the Australian administration and missions had not entered Enga until several generations later, what would they have seen?

References

Arnold, J. E. (ed.) (2005). *Foundations of Chumash complexity* (Vol. 7). Los Angeles: Cotsen Institute of Archaeology.

Arnold, J. E. (2010). The role of politically charged property in the appearance of institutionalized leadership: A view from the North American Pacific Coast. In K. J. Vaughn, J. W. Eerkens and J. Kantner, eds., *The evolution of leadership: Transitions in decision making from small-scale to middle-range societies*, pp. 121–146. Santa Fe, NM: School of Advanced Research Press.

Ballard, C., Brown, P., Bourke, R. and Harwood, T. (eds.) (2005). *The sweet potato in Oceania: A reappraisal* (Vol. 19). Sydney: University of Sydney Press.

Blanton, R. E., Feinman, G. M., Kowalewski, S. A. and Peregrine, P. N. (1996). A dual-processual theory for the evolution of Mesoamerican civilization. *Current anthropology, 37*(1), 1–14.

Boehm, C. (2009). *Hierarchy in the forest: The evolution of egalitarian behavior*. Cambridge, MA: Harvard University Press.

Boone, J. L. (1992). Competition, conflict and the development of social hierarchies. In E. A. Smith and B. Winterhalder, eds., *Evolutionary Ecology, evolution and social behaviour*, pp. 301–337. New York: Aldine de Gruyter.

Bourke, R. M. (2005). Sweet potato in Papua New Guinea: The plant and people. In C. Ballard, P. Brown, M. Bourke and T. Harwood, eds., *The sweet potato in Oceania: A reappraisal*, pp. 15–24. Ethnology Monographs 19. Sydney: University of Sydney Press.

Brennan, P. W. (1977). *Let sleeping snakes lie: A study of central Enga traditional religious belief and ritual* (Vol. 1). Adelaide, SA: Australian Association for the Study of Religion.

Brennan, P. W. (1982). Communication. In B. Carrad, D. Lea and K. Talyaga, eds., *Enga: Foundations for development* (Enga Yaaka Lasemana, Vol. 3). Armidale, NSW: University of New England.

Brookfield, H. C. and White, J. P. (1968). Revolution or evolution in the prehistory of the New Guinea Highlands: A seminar report. *Ethnology, 7*(1), 43–52.

Brown, P. (1970). Chimbu transactions. *Man, 5*(1), 99–170.

Brown, P. (1978). *Highland Peoples of New Guinea*. Cambridge: Cambridge University Press.

Brown, P., Brookfield, H. and Grau, R. (1990). Land tenure and transfer in Chimbu, Papua New Guinea: 1958–1984. A study in continuity and change, accommodation and opportunism. *Human ecology, 18*(1), 21–49.

Brumfiel, E. M. (1992). Distinguished lecture in archeology: Breaking and entering the ecosystem. Gender, class, and faction steal the show. *American anthropologist, 9*(3), 551–567.

Burton, J. (1989). Repeng and the salt-makers: "Ecological trade" and stone axe production in the Papua New Guinea Highlands. *Man, 24*, 255–272.

Bus, G. (1951). The *Te* festival of gift exchange in Enga (Central Highlands). *Anthropos,* 46, 813–824.

Clark, J. E. and Blake, M. (1994). The power of prestige: Competitive generosity and the emergence of rank societies in lowland Mesoamerica. In E. M. Brumfiel and J. W. Fox, eds., *Factional competition and political development in the New World* (Vol. 1), pp. 17–30. New York: Cambridge University Press.

Crumley, C. L. (1995). Heterarchy and the analysis of complex societies. *Archeological papers of the American Anthropological Association, 6*(1), 1–5.

Diamond, J. (2005). Collapse: The dozen most serious environmental problems and what we can do about them. *Skeptic, 11*(3), 36–42.

Earle, T. K. (1997). *How chiefs come to power: The political economy in prehistory.* Palo Alto, CA: Stanford University Press.

Earle, T. K. (2011). Chiefs, chieftaincies, chiefdoms, and chiefly confederacies: Power in the evolution of political systems. *Social evolution & history, 10*(1), 27–54.

Elkin, A. P. (1953). Delayed exchange in Wabag sub-district, central highlands of New Guinea, with notes on the social organization. *Oceania, 23*(3), 161–201.

Faulseit, R. K. (ed.) (2016). *Beyond collapse: Archaeological perspectives on resilience, revitalization, and transformation in complex societies.* Carbondale: Southern Illinois University Press.

Feachem, R. (1973a). The religious belief and ritual of the Raiapu Enga. *Oceania, 43*(4), 259–285.

Feachem, R. (1973b). The Raiapu Enga pig herd. *Mankind, 9*(1), 25–31.

Feil, D. K. (1978). Women and men in the Enga tee. *American ethnologist, 5*(2), 263–279.

Feil, D. K. (1982). From pigs to pearlshells: The transformation of a New Guinea Highlands exchange economy. *American ethnologist, 9*(2), 291–306.

Feil, D. K. (1983). A world without exchange: Millennia and the Tee ceremonial system in Tombema-Enga society (New Guinea). *Anthropos, 78*, 89–106.

Feil, D. K. (1984). *Ways of exchange: The Enga Tee of Papua New Guinea.* St. Lucia: University of Queensland Press.

Feil, D. K. (1987). *The evolution of Highland Papua New Guinea societies.* Cambridge: Cambridge University Press.

Feinman, G. M. (1995). The emergence of inequality: A focus on strategies and processes. In T. D. Price and G. M. Feinman, eds., *Foundations of social inequality,* pp. 255–280. New York: Plenum Press.

Fenton, W. N. (1998). *The great law and the longhouse: A political history of the Iroquois Confederacy* (Vol. 223). Norman: University of Oklahoma Press.

Flannery, K. and Marcus, J. (2012). *The creation of inequality: How our prehistoric ancestors set the stage for monarchy, slavery, and empire.* Cambridge, MA: Harvard University Press.

Frankel, S. (1986). *The Huli response to illness.* Cambridge: Cambridge University Press.

Furholt, M., Grier, C., Spriggs, M. and Earle, T. (2020). Political economy in the archaeology of emergent complexity: A synthesis of bottom-up and top-down approaches. *Journal of archaeological method and theory, 27*(2), 157–191.

Gibbs, P. J. (1977). The cult from Lyeimi and the Ipili. *Oceania, 48*(1), 1–25.

Gibbs, P. J. (1978). The Kepele ritual of the western highlands of Papua New Guinea. *Anthropos, 73,* 434–448.

Glasse, R. M. (1969). *Huli of Papua: A cognatic descent system* (Vol. 8). The Hague: Mouton.

Godelier, M. and Strathern, M. (1991). *Big men, great men: Personifications of power in Melanesia.* Cambridge: Cambridge University Press.

Golson, J. (1982). The Ipomoean revolution revisited: Society and sweet potato in the upper Waghi valley. In A. Strathern, ed., *Inequality in New Guinea Highlands societies,* pp. 109–136. Cambridge: Cambridge University Press.

Graeber, D. (2011). *Debt: The first five thousand years.* New York: Melville House.

Gray, D. (1973). The logic of Yandapu Enga puberty rights and the separation of the sexes. Unpublished MA thesis, University of Sydney.

Guyer, J. I. (1995). Wealth in people, wealth in things: Introduction. *Journal of African history, 36,* 83–90.

Guyer, J. I. and Belinga, S. M. E. (1995). Wealth in people as wealth in knowledge: Accumulation and composition in Equatorial Africa. *Journal of African history, 36,* 91–120.

Harrison, S. J. (2006). *Stealing people's names: History and politics in a Sepik River cosmology* (Vol. 71). Cambridge: Cambridge University Press.

Hayden, B. (1995). Pathways to power. In D. Price and G. Feinman, eds., *Foundations of social inequality*, pp. 15–86. New York: Springer.

Hayden, B. (2001). Richman, poorman, beggarman, chief: The dynamics of social inequality. In G. M. Feinman and T. D. Price, eds., *Archaeology at the millennium*, pp. 231–272. Boston, MA: Springer.

Hayden, B. (2011). Big man, big heart? The political role of aggrandizers in egalitarian and transegalitarian societies. In D. Forsyth and C. Hoyt, eds., *For the greater good of all: Perspectives on individualism, society, and leadership*, pp. 101–118. New York: Palgrave Macmillan.

Hayden, B. (2014). *The power of feasts: From prehistory to the present.* Cambridge: Cambridge University Press.

Hide, R. (2003). *Pig husbandry in New Guinea: A literature review and bibliography.* ACTAR Monograph No. 108.

Hrdy, S. B. (2016). Development plus social selection in the emergence of "emotionally modern" humans. In C. L. Meehan and A. N. Crittenden, eds., *Childhood: Origins, evolution, and implications*, pp. 11–44. School for Advanced Research Advanced Seminar Series. Santa Fe: University of New Mexico Press.

Hughes, I. (1977). *New Guinea Stone Age trade.* Canberra: Department of Prehistory, Research School of Pacific Studies, Australian National University.

Johnson, A. and Earle, T. (2000) *The evolution of human societies: From foraging group to agrarian state.* Stanford, CA: Stanford University Press.

Ketan, J. (2004). *The name must not go down: Political competition and state-society relations in Mount Hagen, Papua New Guinea.* Port Morseby: Institute of Pacific Studies.

Kirsch, P. V. and Rallu, J. L. (eds.) (2007). *The growth and collapse of Pacific island societies: Archaeological and demographic perspectives.* Honolulu: University of Hawaii Press.

Knauft, B. 1990. Melanesian warfare: A theoretical history. *Oceania, 60*(4), 250–311.

Koch, K. F. (1974). *War and peace in Jalemo: The management of conflict in Highland New Guinea.* Cambridge, MA: Harvard University Press.

Kristiansen, K. (1987). From stone to bronze: The evolution of social complexity in northern Europe. In E. M. Brumfiel, T. K. Earle, eds., *Specialization, exchange and complex societies*, pp. 30–51. Cambridge: Cambridge University Press.

Kyakas, A. and Wiessner, P. (1992). *From inside the women's house: Enga women's lives and traditions.* Brisbane: Robert Brown.

Lacey, R. (1975). Oral traditions as history: An exploration of oral sources among the Enga of the New Guinea Highlands. Unpublished PhD thesis. University of Wisconsin.

Lacey, R. (1979). Holders of the way: A study of precolonial socio-economic history in Papua New Guinea. *Journal of the Polynesian Society, 88,* 277–325.

Lacey, R. (1982). History. In B. Carrad, D. Lea and K. Talyaga, eds., *Enga: Foundations for Development*, pp. 8–22. Enga Yaaka Lasemana 3. Armidale: University of New England.

Leach, E. R. (1954). *Political systems of highland Burma: A study of Kachin social structure*. London: Routledge.

Leacock, E. (1978). Women's status in egalitarian society: Implications for social evolution. *Current anthropology, 19*(2), 247–275.

Leahy, M. J. and Crain, M. (1937). *The land that time forgot: Adventures and discoveries in New Guinea*. Funk & Wagnalls.

Lederman, R. (1986). *What gifts engender: Social relations and politics in Mendi, Highland Papua New Guinea*. Cambridge: Cambridge University Press.

Lemonnier, P. (1990). *Guerres et festins: Paix, échanges et compétition dans les Highlands de Nouvelle-Guinée*. Paris: Les Editions de la MSH.

Meggitt, M. J. (1956). The valleys of the upper Wage and Lai rivers, western highlands, New Guinea. *Oceania, 27*(2), 90–135.

Meggitt, M. J. (1958). *Salt manufacture and trading in the western highlands of New Guinea*. Sydney: Australian Museum.

Meggitt, M. J. (1964a). The kinship terminology of the Mae Enga of New Guinea. *Oceania, 34*(3), 191–200.

Meggitt, M. J. (1964b). Male–female relationships in the highlands of Australian New Guinea. *American anthropologist, 66*(4), 204–224.

Meggitt, M. (1965a). *The lineage system of the Mae Enga of New Guinea*. New York: Barnes and Noble.

Meggitt, M. J. and Lawrence, P. (1965b). *Gods, ghosts, and men in Melanesia: Some religions of Australian New Guinea and the New Hebrides*. Oxford: Oxford University Press.

Meggitt, M. J. (1967). The pattern of leadership among the Mae-Enga of New Guinea. *Anthropological forum, 2*(1), 20–35.

Meggitt, M. (1972). System and subsystem: The Te exchange cycle among the Mae Enga. *Human ecology, 1*(2), 111–123.

Meggitt, M. J. (1973). The Sun and the Shakers: A millenarian cult and its transformation in the New Guinea highlands. *Oceania, 44*(2), 109–126.

Meggitt, M. J. (1974). "Pigs are our hearts!" The Te exchange cycle among the Mae Enga of New Guinea. *Oceania, 44*(3), 165–203.

Meggitt, M. (1977). *Blood is their argument: Warfare among the Mae Enga of the New Guinea highlands.* Palo Alto, CA: Mayfield.

Meggitt, M. (1990). Injured husbands and wounded wives: Mae Enga responses to adultery. *Australian Journal of Anthropology, 1*(2), 96–109.

Modjeska, N. (1982). Production and inequality: Perspectives from central New Guinea. In A. Strathern, ed., *Inequality in New Guinea highlands societies*, pp. 50–108. Cambridge: Cambridge University Press.

Nairn, C. (1991). *Ongka's Big Moka (Kawelka).* London: Image Media Services, Granada Television.

Nesse, R. M. (2010). Social selection and the origins of culture. In M. Schaller, A. Norenzayan, S. J. Heine, T. Yamagishi and T. Kameda, eds., *Evolution, culture, and the human mind*, pp. 137–50. Oxfordshire: Psychology Press.

Ostrom, E. (1990). *Governing the commons: The evolution of institutions for collective action.* Cambridge: Cambridge University Press.

Ploeg, A. (1969). *Government in Wanggulam* (p. 228). Leiden: Brill.

Price, T. D. (2021). The emergence of social inequality in prehistory. In O. Cerasuolo, ed.,*The archaeology of inequality: Tracing the archaeological record.* Albany: State University of New York Press.

Price, T. D. and Feinman, G. M. (eds.) (1995). *Foundations of social inequality* (Vol. 1). Berlin: Springer Science & Business Media.

Rappaport, R. A. (1968). *Pigs for the ancestors: Ritual in the ecology of a New Guinea people.* New Haven, CT: Yale University.

Reay, M. (1959). *The Kuma.* Melbourne: Melbourne University Press.

Richerson, P. J., Boyd, R. and Bettinger, R. L. (2001). Was agriculture impossible during the Pleistocene but mandatory during the Holocene? A climate change hypothesis. *American antiquity, 66*(3), 387–411.

Ryan, D. J. (1972). Mok-Ink. In P. Ryan, ed., *Encyclopedia of Papua New Guinea*, pp. 788–789. Melburne: Melbourne University Press.

Sackschewski, M., Gruenhagen, D. and Ingebritsom, J. (1970). The clan meeting in Enga society. In P. Brennan, ed., *Exploring Enga culture: Studies in missionary anthropology.* Wapenanamda: Kristen Press.

Sahlins, M. D. (1963). Poor man, rich man, big-man, chief: Political types in Melanesia and Polynesia. *Comparative studies in society and history, 5*(3), 285–303.

Sahlins, M. D. (1972). *Stone Age economics.* Chicago, IL: Aldine.

Salisbury, R. F. (1962). *From stone to steel: Economic consequences of a technological change in New Guinea.* Melbourne: Melbourne University Press.

Schwab, J. and Gibbs, P. (1995). The Sandalu bachelor ritual among the Laiapu Enga (Papua New Guinea). *Anthropos*, *90*, 27–47.

Sillitoe, P. (1977). Land shortage and war in New Guinea. *Ethnology*, *16*(1), 71–81.

Sillitoe, P. (1979). *Give and take*. Canberra: Australian National University Press.

Stanish, C. (2010). The evolution of managerial elites in intermediate societies. In J. Eerkens, J. Kantner and K. Vaughn, eds., *The evolution of leadership*, pp. 97–119. Santa Fe, NM: SAR Press.

Strathern, A. (1969). Finance and production: Two strategies in New Guinea Highlands exchange systems. *Oceania*, *40*(1), 42–67.

Strathern, A. (1970). The female and male spirit cults in Mount Hagen. *Man*, *5*(4), 571–585.

Strathern, A. (1971). *The rope of Moka: Big-men and ceremonial exchange in Mount Hagen New Guinea*. Cambridge: Cambridge University Press.

Swadling, P., Wiessner, P. and Tumu, A. (2008). Prehistoric stone artefacts from Enga and the implication of links between the highlands, lowlands and islands for early agriculture in Papua New Guinea. *Journal de la Société des Océanistes*, *126–127*, 271–292.

Tainter, J. (1988). *The collapse of complex societies*. Cambridge: Cambridge University Press.

Tuzin, D. (2013). *Social complexity in the making: A case study among the Arapesh of New Guinea*. London: Routledge.

Uchendu, V. C. (1965). *The Igbo of southeast Nigeria*. New York: Holt, Rinehart and Winston.

Vansina, J. M. (1990). *Paths in the rainforests: Toward a history of political tradition in equatorial Africa*. Madison: University of Wisconsin Press.

Vaughn, K. J., Eerkens, J. W. and Kanter, J. (eds.) (2010). *The evolution of leadership*. Santa Fe, NM: SAR Press.

Vicedom, G. F. and Tischner, H. (1943–8). Die Mbowamb, Hamburg (3 vols.).

Waddell, E. (1972). *The mound builders: Agricultural practices, environment and society in the central highlands of New Guinea*. Seattle: University of Washington Press.

Watson, J. B. (1965). The significance of a recent ecological change in the central highlands of New Guinea. *Journal of the Polynesian Society*, *74*(4), 438–450.

Watson, J. B. (1977). Pigs, fodder, and the Jones effect in post-*Ipomoean* New Guinea. *Ethnology*, *16*(1), 57–70.

Wiessner, P. (2001). Brewing change: Enga feasts in a historical perspective (Papua New Guinea). In B. Hayden and M. Dietler, eds., *The archaeological importance of feasting*, pp. 115–143. Washington, DC: Smithsonian Institution Press.

Wiessner, P. (2002). The vines of complexity. *Current anthropology*, *43*, 233–269.

Wiessner, P. (2005). Social, symbolic, and ritual roles of the sweet potato in Enga, from its introduction until first contact. In C. Ballard, P. Brown, M. Bourke and T. Harwood, eds., *The sweet potato in Oceania: A reappraisal*, pp. 121–130. Ethnology Monographs 19. Oceania Monograph 56. Sydney: University of Sydney Press.

Wiessner, P. (2010a). The power of one: Big-men revisited. In J. Eerkens, J. Kantner and K. Vaughn, eds., *The evolution of leadership*, pp. 195–222. Santa Fe, NM: SAR Press.

Wiessner, P. (2010b). Youths, elders and the wages of war in Enga Province, Papua New Guinea: State, society and governance in Melanesia. Discussion Paper, Australian National University, Canberra.

Wiessner, P. (2019). Collective action for war and for peace: A case study among the Enga of Papua New Guinea. *Current anthropology*, *60*(2), 224–244.

Wiessner, P. and Tumu, A. (1998). *Historical vines: Enga networks of exchange, ritual and warfare in Papua New Guinea*. Washington, DC: Smithsonian Institution Press.

Wiessner, P. and Tumu, A. (1999). A collage of cults. *Canberra anthropology*, *22*(1), 34–65.

Wiessner, P. and Tumu, A. (2001). Averting the bush fire day: Ain's cult revisited. In E. Messer and M. Lambek, eds., *Festschrift for Roy Rappaport*, pp. 300–323. Ann Arbor: University of Michigan Press.

Wirz, P. (1952). Quelques notes sur la cérémonie du Moka chez les tribes du Mount Hagen et du Wabaga Sub-district, Nouvelle-Guinée du Nord-est. *Bulletin de la Société Royal Belge d'Anthropologie et de Préhistoire*, *63*, 65–71.

Wohlt, P. (1978). Ecology, agriculture and social organization: The dynamics of group composition in the highlands of New Guinea. Ann Arbor, MI: University Microfilms.

Yen, D. (1974). The sweet potato and Oceania: An essay in ethnobotany. Honolulu: Bishop Museum Bulletin 236.

Young, D. W. (2004). *Our land is green and black: Conflict resolution in Enga*. Goroka: Melanesian Institute Press.

Cambridge Elements ≡

Ancient and Pre-modern Economies

Kenneth G. Hirth

The Pennsylvania State University

Ken Hirth's research focuses on the development of ranked and state-level societies in the New World. He is interested in political economy and how forms of resource control lead to the development of structural inequalities. Topics of special interest include: exchange systems, craft production, settlement patterns, and preindustrial urbanism. Methodological interests include: lithic technology and use-wear, ceramics, and spatial analysis.

Timothy Earle

Northwestern University

Tim Earle is an economic anthropologist specializing in the archaeological studies of social inequality, leadership, and political economy in early chiefdoms and states. He has conducted field projects in Polynesia, Peru, Argentina, Denmark, and Hungary. Having studied the emergence of social complexity in three world regions, his work is comparative, searching for the causes of alternative pathways to centralized power.

Emily J. Kate

The University of Vienna

Emily Kate is bioarchaeologist with training in radiocarbon dating, isotopic studies, human osteology, and paleodemography. Having worked with projects from Latin America and Europe, her interests include the manner in which paleodietary trends can be used to assess shifts in social and political structure, the affect of migration on societies, and the refinement of regional chronologies through radiocarbon programs.

About the Series

Elements in Ancient and Premodern Economies is committed to critical scholarship on the comparative economies of traditional societies. Volumes either focus on case studies of well documented societies, providing information on domestic and institutional economies, or provide comparative analyses of topical issues related to economic function. Each Element adopts an innovative and interdisciplinary view of culture and economy, offering authoritative discussions of how societies survived and thrived throughout human history.

Cambridge Elements ≡

Ancient and Pre-modern Economies

Elements in the Series